The Day's Final Balance

Also by Peter Riley:

Poetry
Love-Strife Machine
The Canterbury Experimental Weekend
The Linear Journal
The Musicians, The Instruments
Preparations
Lines on the Liver
Tracks and Mineshafts
Ospita
Noon Province
Sea Watches
Reader
Lecture
Sea Watch Elegies
Royal Signals
Distant Points
Alstonefield
Between Harbours
Noon Province et autres poèmes
Snow has settled ... bury me here
Author
Passing Measures: A Collection of Poems
The Sea's Continual Code
Aria with Small Lights
Alstonefield (extended edition)
Excavations
A Map of Faring
The Llŷn Writings

Prose
Two Essays
Company Week
The Dance at Mociu

The Day's Final Balance

Uncollected Writings 1965-2006

Peter Riley

Shearsman Books
Exeter

First published in the United Kingdom in 2007 by
Shearsman Books Ltd
58 Velwell Road
Exeter EX4 4LD

www.shearsman.com

ISBN-13 978-1-905700-09-7

ISBN-10 1-905700-09-1

Copyright © Peter Riley, 2007.

The right of Peter Riley to be identified as the author of this work has been asserted by him in accordance with the Copyrights, Designs and Patents Act of 1988. All rights reserved. No part of this publication may be reproduced, stored in a retrieval system, transmitted in any form or by any means, electronic, mechanical, photocopying, recording or otherwise, without the prior permission of the publisher.

Acknowledgements
Some texts included here were originally published as all or part of small books issued by The Curiously Strong, Equipage, Folio (Salt), Grille, The Many Press, Pig Press, The Plague Press, Poetical Histories, and Short Run Press. Texts also appeared in the periodicals *The Ant's Forefoot*, *The Atlantic Review*, *C.C.C.P. 2006*, *Collection*, *Curtains*, *The English Intelligencer*, *The Gig*, *Great Works*, *Grosseteste Review*, *New Directions*, *One*, *The Paper*, *Perfect Bound*, *Spindrift*, and *Turpin*; and in the anthologies *For John Riley* (Grosseteste 1979), *Sneak's Noise* (1998) and *Occasions of Poetry* edited by David Kennedy (Stride 2006).

The publishers and editors of these are warmly remembered and thanked, and apologies made for any publications omitted.

The publisher gratefully acknowledges financial assistance from
Arts Council England.

Contents

Prefatory Note

1. Early poems (1968-72)
   - Introitus — 12
   - Puisque j'ai perdu — 14
   - Two versions — 17
   - Dark Spell — 18
   - Three-part invention for John Dunstable — 19
   - Other Poems Written on 11th May 1968 — 20
   - Comma — 23
   - Minor Thirds — 24
   - Archilochus — 25
   - Wednesday Supermarket Poem(s) — 30
   - The Stones — 31
   - To Live Trying / Let Us All — 32

2. Northern Harbour (1972) — 33

3. Poems written between 1977 and 1994
   - Six Musical Experiences — 44
   - Polecats' Song — 50
   - Wych Elm — 51
   - Elf Shots — 52
   - Essay on the East Window of Killagha Abbey — 54
   - To the tune of "John Riley" — 56
   - After Mandelstam — 58
   - La Sologne 1991 — 59
   - Walking — 60
   - Three Pastoral Poems — 62

4. Floating Verses — 65

5. Royal Signals (1994) — 91

6. Small Square Plots (1996) — 103

7. More and Extra (1992-2002)
    Poems from *Reader / Lecture / Author*   110
    From *Poems to Pictures by Jack Yeats*   118
    Poems extra to *Reader / Lecture / Author*   122
    Poems extra to *Snow has settled ... bury me here*   125
    Prose poems and pieces written
        at the time of writing *Excavations*   128

8. Messenger Street (2001)   133

9. Alstonefield Part VI (2001-02)   139

10. Prose pieces and prose poems (1992-2006)
    Manchester   150
    Alstonefield   158
    Gropina / Leopardi   159
    The Locality   160
    Sant' Alvise   162
    St. Alban's   164
    3rd April 2003   167
    What People Have   168
    [Kemp Town]   169
    Last Bus to Argos   170
    Palladian Abstract   171
    Lorand   172
    Derek Bailey's Funeral   174

11. Carpathian pieces (1999-2004)
    The Lay-by Refreshments Hut   176
    Sunday Evening in Botiza   178
    "I am a Poet"   180
    The BBC at Lunca Ilvei   182
    Two Beggars   185

12. Three walking pieces (2004-05)
    17th November, Youlgrave   190
    Alpine Zones: The Reward   192
    How to get to Ágios Pantaleímon at Boularii   196

13. Poems from abroad (2000-2005)
    Vertigo   200
    "Forgive these warriors..."   201
    Szászcsávás: The Older Stratum   202
    "Long since the stars..."   203
    Pyrenean   204
    Four Transylvanian Songs   205
    Transylvanian Songs   207
    The Children of Maramureş   208

It should be possible to give all poems the title: Reasons for Living Happily.
  Francis Ponge: 'Raisons de vivre heureux'.

Prefatory Note

This book is a collection of pieces in many different genres between poetry and prose, which have never appeared previously in book form and many of which have never been published at all. It excludes the contents of *Love-Strife Machine* (Ferry Press 1969), *The Linear Journal* (Grosseteste 1973), *Lines on the Liver* (Ferry Press 1981), *Tracks and Mineshafts* (Grosseteste 1983), *Snow has settled ... bury me here* (Shearsman Books 1997), *Excavations* (Reality Street Editions 2004), *A Map of Faring* (Parlor Press 2005) and the selected poems *Passing Measures* (Carcanet 2000). It also excludes writings concerning the Llŷn Peninsula in North Wales, which are collected separately. Many pieces, perhaps most, have been altered in the process of transcription, some drastically. The contents of *The Whole Band* (Sesheta 1972) have been rendered down to a set of short poems included in the section *Floating Verses*. *The Musicians The Instruments* (The Many Press 1978) has been reduced to the 'Six Musical Experiences'. The unpublished set 'Northern Harbour' of 1972 had its final poem added in 2005.

A few "versions" from foreign languages are included, which should not be read as anything but derivative poems.

Peter Riley

Early Poems

Introtus

How it begins:
              it begins with me
walking along the shore at Hastings
just short of the surf line, on shingle.

To walk effectively on shingle you have to
lean forwards so you'd fall if you didn't push
your feet back from a firm step down and
back sharp forcing the separate ground
to consolidate underneath you, with a marked
flip as you lift each foot, scattering
stones behind, gaining momentum.

The shore's long and curves
slightly to the south as you approach the bar.
Winter: a hazy, cloudless day
and cold. No horizon to sea.

Looking up from this.
Stopping and raising the head,
correcting the stoop – a
small sea, its sound
on the stones, of the
wash back. Seagulls in winter
lose the harshness of their bark,
more a mewing, and there
aren't many.

It begins and either
stops there or doesn't.

That action, lifting the head,
the skin of the throat unfolding,
air reaching the upper chest
gazing out in no special direction –

position of receptiveness
each sense prepared to act; the body
hearkens – the mind is alerted.

That nothing comes
is good. No news
across the shore is
excellent, the truth
is there for a start.

The flesh is full
of what there is
there / then,
has that, offers
back self, is one
of all that.

And I lean again and
press the stones, bend
homeward, for the door
into what comes,
to bring it further.

Puisque j'ai perdu

Now she cracks hazelnuts on the floor
with a hammer and hands me the kernels
to eat, taste of wood. The town outside
is dark, people are at home. One or two
are bitter-sweet. Yes, some are good
and some are bad. There is music on the radio
by Orlando di Lasso also known as Lassus,
who once sat with William Byrd in a small boat
and they were rowed across the Thames at night.
And all of that is good.

Domini   exaudi
the cat seizes a nut and runs off with it
orationem   meum
the pile of husks on the matting
is greater, at each entry

there is a purity, a goodness:
the generous gift given always calmly
that is my oratio, song and dance
counterpoint and harmony
we stayed up specially for this, it is
my dance tonight, my rhetorick to say
there is a purity which is a goodness
and the generous gift is calmly given
all the time, and I know that out of this
special place it is not given or calm
or good or bad but here it is so utterly
said and heard that it lives on.

The Mass is built on a popular song
which says "Since I have lost" and all the time
in all the specialness we can't omit to notice
that we have also lost, a phrase which is
never far away, tucked into the whole edifice

I am alone, I have lost, I am not what I seem;
indeed we have abandoned and lost so much to be
in this observance together the whole of the earth
and our good sleep, staying specially awake in case
a purity exists by which a gift is given not
necessarily to us but as a giving which exists and
we are forced to recognise against our loss
a constancy.

It is the material of this song, movement and time
breaking into the structure, symmetry encrusted
on stone, the whole theatre of what is set forth
"as if it were natural" reaching to an admission,
that it is ruined in time. The sculpture reverts
to the quarry face: we have lost, we have lost
so much by the time it weaves to an end
that we are hardly where we are and
have donated all our presence into a sung and
danced oratio which reaches its end. Over
the sea or Thames in some dark cave or quarry
is an inscription on a carved tomb
which says again that the utter gift is constant.
Post Scriptum: we have lost.
Appendix: J'ai perdu.

And the gift is of what, of what is,
the human being the person given
to the totality the commonality
given to the continuance over the air beyond
the person in a grand manner of perception,
and here also the enclosure of house, room,
group of two assuming ourselves into the future
by a child, so given entire with a clause in
small print: we also lose, we must, otherwise
these things made are of such

colossal beauty these masses tombs and
mutual percepts we might petrify on the spot,
we'd have nothing at all.
A particle, or seed, remains, "lost"
to the immediate city and
isn't this how we survive, how we survive
our own generosity and purity, isn't this
our mark of love?

Seafront
After Montale[1]

The wind is getting stronger, the darkness
ripped to shreds, your shadow on a thin fence
screwed up and thrown away. Too late now

to want to be yourself. A rat clumping
down a palm-tree, lightning on the fuse,
lightning on the long lashes of your stare.

Poem
After Machado[2] *in the Chinese manner*

Purple Twilight Embers smoulder
through Black Cypress Grove.

Fountain in Dark Arbour of Columns
with Stone Cupid naked

Silent dreaming. In Marble Bowl
Water lies dead.

---

[1] Lungomare, in *La bufera e altro* (1956)
[2] "Las ascuas de un crepúsculo morado...", *Del camino, Poesías completas* (1933) XXXII

Dark Spell
after Francis Ponge[1]

When the foreground more than the distance becomes dark and after a long time of funereal day-dreaming the rain beating the earth black & blue quickly establishes mud, a pure gaze worships it: that of the sky already on its knees again on this slimy body broken under the wheels of enemy carts in the long gaps of which however from a teal to its obstinate ford constancy and liberty guide our steps.

---

[1] Sombre période, in *Liasse*, (1942)

Three-Part Invention for John Dunstable

1. The spirit   gives off daylight   the Father of
2. Comes down,   the dew   from
3.   Creation: the

Equity   comes quietly,   the taker   spreads concord over
                  the   sky
gift   given   as easy as breath

the fields   comfort   over ice   :rest in work
                     as a blessing   man to god or the earth
o u t   freely   the fountain or   fire of love

the light in the breasts of the company of the hopeful   / Without
as a form of protection to the mind   / lost
where promise lies   in the hand   and speech   / a star

this   nothing   will wash clean   make fertile
                    without   home   or   consolation
   in   the   farthest   reaches   of   love   a con-

         unfreeze   strengthen   fill the company of men
the condition sways,   re-forms   due to death   forgiven
    cord   that can   in strength   move   we need

with safety   that   heavens   rejoice.
purified   led   towards   the city.
    help   to know   the child   and trust   always.

Other Poems Written on 11th May 1968[1]

1.
And right through the day that gentle murmur
as of any metropolis, and this is a big town. Open
the window and it's there. A seagull gliding over
a block of flats on the horizon. When you look for them
they're always there, among and above the buildings,
careful watchers, scouring the surfaces, captains of distance.

Stink of summer and murmur of traffic.
Time children, these things inhabit us,
whispering behind us as it's the baby's
bed-time again, threat and promise, loss
of self, murmurs of a gratified old age
moving to and from us with the tide.

2.
Only a week after their last cleaning the window
glass begins to salt over, takes a white coat
from the sea mists and vapour in the wind.

The materials of the universe are alive and active.
Something very questionable floats in from the
kitchen and the heart defends its grip.

3.
One of the screws I took out of the window frame
because spring has arrived, lies on the table.
The thread is corroded, the body stained,
and the head bright where the pressure of at least
two screwdrivers held by two people who

---

[1] Twenty poems written on 11th May 1968 are in the book *Love-Strife Machine* (1969)

will never meet, has shaved off slivers and
dust of steel, wearing the groove almost away.
One such sliver hangs now, from the scarred
edge. It can't be used again.

4.
Something follows me round the house,
something difficult to avoid, a kind of
dogged angel inscribed "Why don't you just
stop messing around and get on with something?"

I've tried all sorts: amateur theatricals, stamp collecting,
19th Century symphonies, editing magazines,
taking long walks over the mountains and stomach ulcers.

And poverty. Adrienne says I'm getting
that lost look about the eyes, of the really poor.
Well, senses of exclusion and privileged want
are always attractive, and comforting, but
the only real thing is the cause at the centre.

Cause to be listened to. This person in the room
makes me nervous, that I try to
satisfy on the page, this
tongue of fire, that hardly notices I'm here.

5.

We don't belong in language, it's
a foreign mode. It's night now,
and the curtains are drawn. The old woman
in the flat underneath will be asleep

so I mustn't play records. I glare
at the silence, the town heterophony
muffled behind the curtains. Language is a distinct
enemy–we have instruments–we have
taken each other prisoner, and now we want the truth.

Old woman sleep calm, old
truth keep us at it.

6.

Whatever you do is right.
Whatever you say is true.

Whatever you are, exists.

Comma

A van rings its bell in the courtyard. The new flat
bare and quiet, the bright poster on the wall,
a black and white wooden horse carrying ten children.
There are windows onto the courtyard and windows
the other side onto the busy road, muffled behind
Venetian blinds and double glass.
The town is full of Christmas lights in the early dark.

The road leads to the town centre, we take a bus.
Half way there it cuts through an elongated park
that curves right across this side of town,
a long strip of grass edged with trees,
a lake and children's swings. We get off there.

It is cold, a fast wind brushes the lake
the trees darken and shake, they fret
their hard cold branches against each other.
The traffic slides past at the distant crossing.
Laden clouds pass over the top. My son
uses the swings and slides contentedly, we get
a bus back. We hope to pay our fares
without having to speak.

We get back to the same bare room, one table
and three chairs and we have dinner of the unusual
foods the local supermarket provides, where
you can buy without speaking.
We put him to bed in this foreign place.

Let us not become familiar, never know
where we are so well we forget, let us be
always these bemused arrivals staring like
refugees at the parks and houses not knowing
what is expected next or what will stay.
At the centre is a cathedral, and another day.

Minor Thirds: song pieces after Boris Vian

1.
Your hand in mine,
your body in our bed,
your breath mixed in mine,
living turned chordal.

2.
Through the day's obscurity she burns,
through failed languages and the constant
drone that penetrates the window-frames
she burns like a lamp in the night
somewhere close to the sea.

She burns like a red fire
beyond parked lorries at the roadside.

3.
Sky streaked with rain and wind
weighs on the dull fields,
birds fly over the pond.
Love catches on your shoulder ahead of me –
your grey scarf in the vast cold landscape
that curves round us all the time
like a knowing tourist.

4.
Snow is falling. Are we
as we were and shall we remain?
Who knows. It is here,
my heart packed in your hands.

5.
Anxiety settles.
Last glimpse of a fast car oxidising.

Archilochus: The complete fragments

Disgraced:
    left my sword by a bush, damn it
but I saved my skin
       I'll buy another one just as good when I

face-saving, it's my *règle de vie*
This is what I said to her:

The "opinions" people "have" of me—
how can you propose that?
All I do is borrow what I can use
though I love where I'm loved, hate my enemy
the dead rats of the world

A voice told me: return to the city
these sea-battles are doing you no good,
find your strength in the city
reign there, exercise your power
be admired

And I find you again, back here
after that long journey on a small ship
victim of nothing and nobody, I'm glad.
Me, I came here wanting mainly a good woman,
I'd already taken her by the hand
and we were on our way to her place when I remembered my cargo

it was lost
    irrecoverable
the sea had it all.
You have survived the war, you stayed alive.
And you've kept your youth. A god has guarded you.
I've fallen on bad times again and here I am

dedicated to solitude, slipping into obscurity . . .
though I was promised to the light

        she likes to walk around with a sprig of myrtle
        over her shoulder so the flowers augment her hair,
        shadowing the nape and shoulders

(now) that the smoke of braziers rises all over the town again
(another war)

        guard your serenity
           the earth, spread with blood
              the long ships

well, at the heart of discord even the worst scoundrel
picks up a few bits of humour

Death as a gift
                people are dying of hunger in this city
        they should understand

me, not in the least surprised
if suddenly the deer prefer
the sonorous waves to the land
and swop pasturage with the dolphins
    while they hole themselves up in the hills

        Archeanactides

        the son of

arranging his wedding

he calcinates

Why have you nipped the cricket in its wing?

      was transported / in sheer joy (of the act)
      like a wind on the (coastal) rocks
      (she) beat her wings and took flight

Then on that good soil they established
a new place to inhabit, and cleared new fields;
emigrés of so many lands, unnoticed in the world
but, with some god's help
this island should be theirs

   that thin boat tossing on the sea
DO SOMETHING I yelled,
slacken the ropes, catch the right gust
or something, we'll remember you
get us through this and your name will stay with us
   I said to the man

season follows season, time
extends itself
      I no longer seek your door

I'm not concerned about Gyges and his treasury.
I was never given to envy and I don't get emotional

about the administration.
Power of empire, where is it?
Miles from my eyes

like the spine of an ass, the island rears up out of the sea
with its coronet of wild forest

not such a handsome place, not so desirable
as the banks of Siris

        remember I too can belt out the song of Dionysus
        the dithyramb
        if I've had enough to drink

to forget Pharos, the island, its glum fig-trees and the life there
dragging waves

        promised, to the light/

and I find *you*
                your serenity
   like the wind on
        rocks, season follows season
     émigré
         it was lost:

my shield, now gracing some foreign war-effort
a beautiful weapon
            I left it by a bush
But I saved my skin

My heart, confounded in an endless series of insoluble problems,
renew yourself, offer resistance, offer them a resistant heart.
Don't flinch at evil,
in gaining don't exult, in losing don't tremble
supine at home–savour success, lament misfortune but not to
　　excess,
learn the rhythm which governs human life.

Wednesday Supermarket Poem(s)

Everywhere you go here you get
Herb Alpert and his Tijuana Brass,
pumping away like rubber kittens.

I sit in the supermarket coffee-bar
Wednesday morning as usual. I read
The New American Poetry

and the labels on the sugar cubes.
They recommend themselves in remote
languages. The coffee is very good.

It is bright here, it is modern, it is bright red
and bright modern, it seems to work well
and how did I get from here to

The rose is a prismatic breaking of light
violent without harm, reached through
conflicts unknown in pure red bars.

The Stones

There are not so many questions.

What does constitute the good movement?

Picking an old man up off the stones is a movement of celestial scope. If it is not he might as well stay there. He'll end up there one day. Celestial moans. Petrific bones. And without picking old men up off stones no heavenly box is worth the postage on it. The stones are natural objects.

To Live Trying

To love as the leaf turns
into itself at each station
of the year and casting
a glance behind they
wait, the four of them:
him, her, the other and the
child much more than promise.
Day can no longer be checked.
Luna Park is closed.

Let Us All

The rose turns spiral,
demands more light from
sky to sky it is
lost above and an honest button
is deeper in love, much
further into music.

Decline to surrender
the foolish grin in your hand.

Northern Harbour

1.

Paled in matchless retract he has
fallen away from her to a valley
heavy with crosses who was
so trusted, and now estranged gives
birth to his mother on the distant couch
unnoticed, purple flowers
beside him nodding on their
stems as the world will have it so.
In what state or power he could become
kind he does not know, dismembered by
lotus ants for the sake of development
breaking athwart the green cleft and
occluded wavelength he thought he
want this pre-human clarity.

2.

But the image box was only on hire and once
alone it is night, the earth indicates
its preference for the lost and faithful
while he, shrugged out of the light, cowboy
sabbath in ruins and the cold lizard
deafens at his feet. Outpatienced he is
scared to look her in the eyes for the true
horizon is there, in that arc kept, thickening
to cloudy blue beyond the forked inlet.
Well or ill he traces his fault, his razor
snags on the morning soap and
opens an ancient track through fields
of cowslips, sunken to flint, down-
hill everway.

3.

Grounded, and the stream is not clear
and the notch in the skyline fills with snow,
our daily fuse-box, we are half
asleep, forgive us, our daily refusal.
Then lights enter the bay as a signal
long attended, moontrack vibrating on the
stave the choirboy's cue a wooden rod
heading for Vivaldi's foot. A wasp falls
disbanded through the black air, the youth that
emerges in the middle of a life nameless and
meaning no harm but far too late the nerves
connect, the sides touch, he floats howling
out of the window curves over the hill and wakes
up every sleeping vole on the island.

4.

Christmas token at the cottage door, the map
was mapped for the faithful he is
lost on a black moor or study table waiting
for the star to enter its place in the heart
the hole where the stone used to be.
He is in his chair and the wish waits
in its rusty trap. His offer calculates
while he dozes. His ignorance falters,
flutters in the elements and settles
on someone's shoulder at last. He opens
the door, the night takes his hand
the coin in his palm turned
upwards. Damage laid into the distant
future the hypothesis grinds on.

5.

The bedrock sparkled,
a nightchild came shout-
ing at six the imp-
ending reversals:
hedges aflame with
desire come together
past any wish on the
empty page forever.
Take it in the yellow cup
reluctant as normal,
for the world captains
figured this out
long ago
and called it waste.

6.

Just where the wine is
deepest he walks out
thinking something
needs to be done with these
stacks of surplus affection piled
open on his knowledge of the world.
Mother sends him out for
fish and chips if he returns
with a crown he must be a thief.
But he thought his offer was
black and white and it seemed
like socialism turned
down for advantage, not
for the world will he forget

7.

To keep steady and point
to the farm on the cliff
created as it is in space
as the third space between us
full of worth, the unsold fruit
we follow with our eyes
all the way to the boiler room.
By trust postponed the house is
vacuumed now, the light burns
grey in the fields scattered with
rosebay fluff and bits of fuse-wire,
cancelled gardens with leaning
sheds. Unexpected trope, prize
virgin forehead, undisclosed.

i.

The tongues of flame around your waist
are cold to the touch and new breezes
laden with yellow dust arise from
tombs of kings, we cough our way
through to night. Cancellation
of theory, under the banked and
calling stars pale lines on the earth
pass by the megalith and
down the fields to fields of
shifting grain. Shifting gain
falls from my arm as it rises
to the cheekbone, ashen tissue
that marks me sinking to you,
winding roads I never dreamt

ii.

To know you now I enter a state
of columns, arches, vaults, ruins
of a night and its unmanaged hopes
to continue through any makeshift
dwelling, cosy domestic or costly
protective, charcoal grey.
In a leather wallpapered coffee-bar
with a glass of very cold milk it is
possible to mention the future
and look neither up nor down.
Those to whom we mean something,
spirits we grazed in the open fields
now pass silently in the street
together will time make all things right?

iii.

Drink up and go, we engaged ruin,
turned our days into warnings
and lost the prospectus in the
cold breezes of dawn between
blocks of flats, slowly labouring
the cold pavement to reach
a bungalow with a fridge and cans
of condensed milk in a cupboard.
Small rodents begging recognition
scuttle into the bank, sure at least
of their names. But I was he
and you and you were she or them
if I was him or any
of the four were us.

iv.

As anyone nested in the armchair of
radical but entirely self-fulfilling
action his glance will ever stray,
assuming terminal points, glitter
on a long black dress no woman ever
wore and areas of cloud fuzz
over, two hands on her waist.
Parents will keep children
from the light in their heads,
red and orange, of the year, show them
the ships in the bay but never
the ticket itself, the naked almanac –
there are no guides to love,
or histories of wrong.

v.

Innocence appears disguised as soldiers or
young girls and rips apart the baptistery.
A torpedo packed with sugared almonds
makes for the pier where Jackson's Follies
are waiting to go on with the Funeral Dance.
Innocence arrives in the form
of a look of dazed trust on someone's
face and the whole circus calls it
a day and goes home singing.
The constant bud rocked in
opaque tides survives ages and persons,
ambition and despair, survives body
fluids and uniforms and moves into
meaning sailing forth.

vi.

Ordinary days
begin here and
inhabit this glow
with increasing
relief as it deepens
and darkens over
the town, lights
enter the bay,
take her
down the hill
to the point of highest incidence,
the angle at A,
take her
to the highest harbour.

vii.

Or, sweet comrades, now
that trust is riven
by opportunity into heart
rending waste shall we settle
down to a lifetime's work?
Shall we, stitch and sow
or weep and crow or be
the heroes of our own
uncertainties? It strikes
ten, turn and
look back, that
old man at the gate
full of awesome gift
ours for the asking.

8/viii

People who don't and perhaps
never will exist
tend the ground between us,
their faint falling cries
in wild forsaken places where
the rotten wood leans
against the wall. There
the ring passes to earth
burnished at the field edge
and carolled into years O listen
to the modest and reasonable plea
at the back of the funeral hall, the
wrapped present glowing with certainty,
the creak of the closing book.

1977-1994

Six Musical Experiences[1]

1. Derek Bailey (Guitar)

Starting from everything we could possibly have been doing a line tends out in the morning hurt, a sustained spark. A quiet and lonely thing in the grey forests of the world.

As far as to the fringes of beyond us a lamp on the horizon scores its intentions as inexorable, starting to turn towards us. Electric or elastic suspension starting from an arrow-shot. Listen, it wavers and dies.

The path closes behind the light. And it multiplies and disperses, opening into a spread, a box, a bedsittingroom in the mountains, we are drawn in its trail and cowboys and falconers turn towards us as we pass by and the moon sets before us and hermits leap out of tombs in the cliff face and read us treatises of love and death, and up there on the far plateau is a plate of light, spreading . . .

The broadening of the world in our absence, affection hovering over the well squawking with hunger while we drink and fade.

Techniques for keeping the flame alive, the sound in the air against the inertness of matter. Continual praise, the faithful orisons every day in tiny chapels on remote Irish headlands, cupping the fire or burning the flag . . .

Wound music. And the vast solitude in the echo, threading the streets looking for a partner, the spaces between the musicians full of invisible fire.

It also hurts, moving towards and away from us and the world. Let it hurt, it doesn't matter.

Nothing else matters.

2. Han Bennink (percussion)

When you hit the trees
the leaves drop off.
You collect feathers.

Slowly something, a feather or a leaf, flutters down
and hits the pavement with a deafening crash.
A defining crash.

The shock, and persistence,
of sheer gentleness, the
unrelentingly human, the
cutting and stroking edge
of anything that's sheer

And surrounds us
and breaks through all our delays
as waving logs we drive full-tilt into the snowbank.

---

[1] These are redacted from *The Musicians The Instruments* (The Many Press, 1978) a rather outrageously convoluted set of pieces in homage to the musicians taking part in a kind of improvisers' symposium called Company Week organised by Derek Bailey in London in 1977. A second edition modified towards readability appeared in *Six Poets: Views & Interviews* (The Gig 2001).

3. Maarten van Regteren Altena (bass)

Through the heart-holes of our corpses when we turn the handle
   we witness a clown show,

a mime, a puppet theatre, in dim flickering where Laurel and
   Hardy get trapped in all the fine objects we've invented and
   fall over in tears.

The tears are real: a dew on the lens, which casts our vision like a
   fly's all round us to the world

in bits, in clarity,
we recognise the graceful stupidity
of our survival. The simplicity
of our complexions.

4. Tristan Honsinger ('cello)

As if your life depends on it?

Play as if our lives depend on it.

Not on its urgency, but on its being there,

a bastion of sound between us and wrong,

cohered by speed.

5. Steve Lacy (soprano saxophone)

Carefully, feeling the way, like a slug, testing the ground with our horns, retracting and proceeding, and, as the day gathers force, opening out, breathing in a wider and wider landscape. The full and chiming biomental sphere, bright with trees and mice and nesting orioles . . .

Song at the pitch of hunger, the blackbird in the late evening, breaking his time across the stones of the valley by the slight rain for the truth of it, lost for the furtherance . . .

This "we" is no more than a trust, and an audience.

And the mice, what about the mice? They are gnawing holes in our hearts,

To let through the light.

6. Toy Instruments

We are caught in a commerce
And wring our fingers:
The nurse is terse
And the gypsum lingers.

The examination
Is only a game
That starts at the end
And begins again.

So play with the toys
That reflect the stars
And suffer the noise
That bites at its bars.

Like a broken clock
In a school of music,
Smiling back
At whoever views it.

Father has locked
In stone and bricks
The key to the clocks
And covered with sticks

The hole to the heart
Secure from rival.
We're waiting to start.
Method: survival.

Polecats' Song[1]

What is wrong
With sitting long
Waving your tongue
At a passing song?

What is right
About staying up all night
Trying to fight
The absence of light?

> What's the matter
> With the hurried hatter?
> Toast on batter
> Would make him fatter.
>
> What's amiss
> With an honest kiss
> Against the hiss?
> Think about this.

What is so
Wherever you go
Is how you know
The glow of snow
Will never leave
The back of your sleeve
If you believe it.

---

[1] In the narrative from which it is extracted, this song is sung by two polecats, North Polecat and South Polecat, in a clearing in the forest on the Equator, to the accompaniment of small percussion instruments.

Wych Elm

Be home soon. Me buries head in fire
but the new mum's trace calls me to tasks
and the kitchen situation comes for me like
a backing lorry, dishes and ice soaring at
brink of dump. I deflect into the garden.
It's fairly sparse, and the feathered protegées
crouch under the cypress, witholding
more eggs. Beyond this suspension
is a new town over the mountains,
a town of ash crystals, strata of tense,
in danger of being quarried away before
I get there to resurface any already
adequate road to here. I couldn't stand
the trace if you were layered beyond
earshot for a filthy peace. Remember
finely as the day descends how love
set out by the edge of a broad and
feral highway, guided by a dim la-
trine-like star whereso the driver's going,
it hardly mattered. Casting for sign of
fruition meets opposition competition
and beauty, honestly together. Favour treads
the causeway of a concentric camp ever
more the guard of joy's reward and bone's
an intervallic fence at flesh's edge.
Then I close the door, to find the kitchen.
Another stiller simmering landscape I'd
not expect, where the bargain can only be
struck again, just as the distant ridgelight
seals it for the route home, the very forge
of constancy to cloak our blood in
uniform wing, black for the sufferance
by a white tile. The voters clamour for a slice:
to hell with them. The present calls.
Oh both of you, be home soon.

Elf Shots

Now the table is set, a covenant to endure
through heart of now and wish to be
devoutly even, even as my lips hurt today;
it has all been bought with means.
Now the table's laid I can't leave it,
tea towel over my shoulder like a loose
bra strap, guardian of this vale where
we try not to be eaten by the food, not
too much. The divinity of that certainly
isn't prudential, in fact the whole band
knows itself by its good appetite and
how openly it closes; local time
or motherlove brought to conclusions
sealed under the inverted teacups to
make possible what is lived: a new love
not transferred from anywhere, peculiar in
every facet to us, and is itself that which
concludes the foregone mysteries, complete
or not, this thick new life is the lid.
Oh clamp it constantly at the forge of
constancy, otherwise this holy day is
pure bank, our very care of the child trans-
gressed into fear for the deposit. For even
as the hedges darken and speedwell and concrete
glow in dim patches still is the traveller
attended, through magnetic garden and
retail glade a human spark struck off
the fossil shells darts over and back
tracing the head arch, wild on
hymen's shore my God behind me entirely
to come, the moon and its fall. This cuts
the oil routes. The layers of blame break
at veins and bridges across which
your heart is plainly mine, just
a little pecked en route. Very lust,
cloaked in tar, is our frontier man

and the wish its own sufficient caution
as messenger from the sky cists wanting us
home. Pavilions and abattoirs beam with
gain below the town and rail trucks
clank in the night – who would claim the least
victory or any redemption from the state we
all inhabit like something fallen from a lorry.
Victims, losers, we come back talking of
truth meaning only you and I love this
earth we die of, the human garden set aslant
the starry gradients, the scarred night.
Trim the border as you reach it to the ghosts
of outside, usufruct; guard that and the house
is ready. The kettle steams forth, light on
the far hill concertinas, the butter holds
its breath, the bread stretches to Hell.
Yes, we shall be even. Sit down and fall to.

Essay on the East Window of Killagha Abbey

Uncertain and yet managing the journey,
able to return and tell, if only an echo
or shadow of what he had seen, what
he had seen through. He's up there on the
eminence now, telling it all. It snaps behind
him and recysts into time, and really what
's left? We pay, settle down, check knife
fork spoon, switch off the main light. He
persists. He won't have it any more closing
on its own vector . . . He shifts northwards
into the beam. We begin to see through him.

> Look, there is no such thing, no self
> land; you recognise your terminal as
> the heartneedle spins. There are points of
> light in the water of the rotting deep and
> you sail over on a tin tray smeared with
> currency as long as it holds. Then you are set
> forth into love where the contraries touch
> in closing distance, which ends us.
> Surely the rising sun is constant, it is
> our postmark as we walk again the thin line
> of gathered debris to where we are.

Telling-it-all, which is only another and
complete departure from here where nothing
but the skeletal body remains to be said,
hardly worth an ear. Truly the flesh
is blown off him onto the east wall, the map
writhing in the heat cuts perspex frontiers
across the heartspace, against the vein, purpose
burning blue to the final signature: green
ideograms on the white sand, where horse and
rider passed in the night. Such solitude
burns across the earth towards us

and arrives to be taken under the arm:
a calm, not a residue or a fall but an actual
trade. Orange and blue-green lichens spread
over the stonework. Such is the journey, wall
to wall, ground in, intercepted at truth.
Night by day the cavities in the graveyard
transmit their messages across our workspace.
We stand at the entrance, a tree of petal flames
in front of us through which the sky is this
and that, darker and lighter than it was but always
parcel to our furthest wish we are completely
determined, to finish.

To the Tune of "John Riley"[1]

Comes back together,
    the wholly distant,
Comes back to land
    against the cry:
How shall we know him
    when the pain is missing
And when the fires turn
    back to their sky?

Bring him in quickly
    or drink the powder,
Bring him in scarcely
    and shade his eye
Which hovers over
    our loves remaining;
Did you not hear his
    intricate sigh?

Calling us into
    a strict mutation
Wide as the band
    the starlings ply;
This is the order
    of a homely nature
Wrenched in the fault a-
    cross his reply.

Now that we live with
    his hunger's essence
Under the moon where
    the truth's a lie,
We have him daily
    about his business,
Sharpening the need to
    wish him good-bye.

[1] Written on the death of the poet John Riley as a contribution to his memorial anthology. The melody is traditional.

After Mandelstam[1]

Pure clear cups
The noble harmony and deep peace
Of my household gods set
Aside from sidereal pitch.

My household gods, always still,
Rapt in scrupulous niches,
As the sun dims and thought extends
I listen to their silences.

What toy destinies
What timid laws
These finely sculpted bodies decree,
Cold and fragile.

There are gods needing no worshipping,
You and the god are equal.
Your painstaking hand is permitted
To move them from one place to another.

[1] The seventh poem of *Stone* (1913).

La Sologne 1991

The day goes through its language forward
I meet it in the evening when it turns at last
to face me beside the lake in the forest
closing its eyes at the simplest point,
two ducks on the water, two herons
floating high in the sky like black twigs
two pains in one breast,
two grey eyes that set the day at rest.

The days turn through their volume onward
surer than hand or dream or any damaging thing
to reach the lake in the forest
and close the story at its fullest hour,
two ducks on the water, two herons
floating high in the sky like black pigs
one pain in two breasts the heart turning to face
the night of two grey eyes that saved the day.

Walking

I remember what it was like, walking across the land,
The long roads you covered for days with
Nothing to hear but birds and trees, occasional
Tractors ploughing the land and the wind blowing
Kind or cruel as the wind blows and sometimes
It rained and you got soaked as you walked in those
Old macks that absorb water but chances were
You walked on in the wind and dried out before
You stopped for the night, you stopped at inns
Or in good weather lay under a hedge to rouse
At dawn as the sharp faint light spread sideways
Across the fields droplets gleaming on the leaves
And ate your bread and cheese for breakfast and
Shat behind a tree and walked on over the next
Hill along the next valley for the next day or
Over the plains between the wheat fields from
Village to village crossing rivers by bridges
And fords, no special equipment needed you just
Put on your mack and grabbed a little rucksack
And walked out of your house to get a bus or
Train to somewhere you could walk, on the paths or
Roads as you needed to, not many vehicles around,
Quiet landscapes, but there used to be a lot of
Bird song in the air in those days and when
You got to villages they were usually busy specially
At weekends and after school when the children
Were playing and shouting on the green, these days
The villages and fields everywhere are silent but for
A constant slight grumbling from the sky you could
Buy food from houses and farms, you lived off
Pieces of bread, cheese, apples, chocolate and
Evening dinners at pubs it was a very good way of
Enjoying yourself on a small income you could
Do it for two or three weeks at a run whenever
You were free though spring and autumn were best

And my word how you could think on those walks!
The mind free of avoidance and resentment ambled
Far off on its own in logical steps and sudden leaps
Like someone clearing a stream as you walked on
Hearing and seeing everything and you nodded
To the people you passed, dwellers in farms villages and
Small towns who were, what shall I say, locals
In a way they no longer are, well they were likely
To speak to you given a chance they were
Always interested in someone from somewhere else
You didn't want to buy their homes and they
Weren't going to talk television but you'd follow
Together the graceful discourses and gentle hopes
Of early socialism in a friendly sparring match
Between news of wars and horses, as you drank
The fresh ale in a village inn to end the day
Alone swaying up wooden stairs to a room with a small
Wood fire in the grate and a window under the eaves
Opening onto total blackness and silence, the
Country night in its usual persistent force.
I remember doing this out of sheer pleasure and a sense
Of partaking of breadth, but also persistently
Grasping an opportunity, as if it were bound to end.

Three Pastoral Poems
in Donegal 1994

Corkerbeg 1 : The Neighbour

The goats eat everything, have you seen
the goats today, could you tell me
which field they're in?

They have stripped the lower branches
of the trees outside my house

The cuckoo on the corner tree my alarm clock
the beating of the snipe my evening bell

Alone and melancholy for many weeks
especially in the long winters

Neither winning nor losing
I attach a cup to the spring.

Nancy's Bar

"I was a soldier in Belfast for four years"
and suddenly the bar was empty

We also
tire ourselves

and tired of proof, tired
of acknowledgement

move out
even of the short song

and the beautiful quiet talk.
Galleon starfield.

Corkerbeg 2: Hedge School

Air courses down from the mountain
across the lightly constructed space
left to right   tired but adamant
to teach adequacy   light from dark things

Cold in the walls, the wine of age
the lost masquer settles down for good
bends forward to feed the small fire

Waterlogged ground, cross slabs on back field knolls,
far from advancement or delay
women and young children
hitch-hike without fear.

FLOATING VERSES

the collection of very small poems
1963-2003

Cumberland 1957

Lakes are to mountains
As flutes are to gongs.

Instruction

Stop it and give yourself
To the weather.

The Stately Fountains

One, any one of the sparrows
surging over the square (actually
they were starlings) will
have its say and the sky
is pink to the left, a rose
presented personally
to each dream-wrapt citizen,
and to the right, blue.

Against Betjeman

A back garden in Slough, a young woman
sits on a kitchen chair under a tree,
suckling a baby.
This is what is happening in Slough.

Hastings

A window opening onto a cliff-side
where cats play in the grass.

Hora

The eternal round dance in the circular enclosure:
cosmic support for the Act of 1801
while the sky constantly shifts its patterns
into novelty. The golden ring is never
a structure. I would follow the force
of its first making at the forge of industry
and compassion.

Mr Churchill[1] said (yesterday) that death
is not *experienced* by the self but only
observed in the other and therefore
we are eternal because
we shall never experience death.
But I think this might be a sleight-of-hand
since we also don't experience falling-asleep
but we get very tired.

[1] (R.C. Churchill, literary critic, not Winston)

No hopers

Dada dada dada
Beckett Kerouac Cage
we are *taught* to distrust
skilful observation careful thought
and the peaceful eating of biscuits
but then we have to go we
have to have to go.

RCC on death, cf. Wittgenstein, *Tractatus*
6.43111. I still think it's a sleight-of-hand
exactly in the way our visual field has no limits
except, we live on the earth,
eternal except we die.

Untrustworthy practitioners

How can they live
wedged into the curve of the embankment
as if the threat were not personal
and febrile extension served
against the creatures of fire?

Hedgehog

It isn't true: we can start
right from the centre, plain
excitement and trace its course on
that basis: because it is all
ours and we owe nothing
to the world to make us
abandon that prize for some
apparently bigger shift.

Brighton and Hove

Freight cars clatter in the night.
I tell you this: they are going
to London slowly and their wheels are the vortices
of a commerce none of us shall ever touch.

Very little remained

Soft light of morning
Soft warning light
Across the world
You could eat it, no?

Faint hope

Appropriate linguistic usage
Might earn for some of us again
A cup of bread or a bough of pain,
Appropriate linguistic usage.

Odense

Apples, cow-bells, tin-openers and silk scarves
piled up in the hall. What we were
has just arrived, do we want it?

After / for Peter Baker

Sunlight on the
red binding opening
to the page itself,
burning blue
with no flame

Seems more
certain
than the certainty
of everything

Fragments of a book

1.
Night, dark and
snow outside. We
joke to each other.

2.
Your cuticle particularly fair,
your demeanour or comportment
welcoming and totally involved,
your repetitions mine.

3.
When the green overcoat covers us all
we can pick and choose what we like but for now
we act in accordance and suffer no delay.

4.
Every gesture, every movement of the lip
pours to my head enveloped in
rays of light. Screaming down
the curve the star is nowhere now
because of day.

5.
Mutual assent carefully
preserved and nourished
into a habitable condition:
a row of very ordinary houses
containing more exciting proposals
than anything in your head.

6.
We pause on the edge of the city,
stripes on the surface of the eye

caused by daylight and distance,
blind-stamped: with care
embossed: with love.

Bird song in slow dawn:
Exquisite hunger bounded by trust.

Forego the luxury of doubt:
Permit the fear
To radiate against the bone.

Across the axis
Of the dark machine
a small song.
Plum blossom trapped in the sky.

In dream I seem
late, to see you
compass the sphere
in a slight lapse.

Cheshire grim

A cold and feeble wind passes
though my father's house:
the heart void of speech,
the mouths silently flapping.
The listeners shake their heads
and pick up crumbs from the carpet.

And outside
the slow silk of people
at peace about their business
ruffles the day to music.

The star is nothing now the day echoes
clear over distance
protected by song.

Instruction revoked

Consort together
Whatever the weather.

Sailing home

Held in the boat as in the hand of my own feelings!

So many belle-lettrist clichés apply
with particular poignancy to so much of my life.

He sings with his ship.

Reader

So much future percolates from you,
future newsreels flicker in your eyes,
birds flying, coal

runs through you
demanding satiety
and a name.

───────────────

Oh what endhood, to be
monstre gai, to stammer
again and again: wish,
wish, peace, bone.

───────────────

Through field and forest

An elegant and inspiring landscape
Marred only by dangerous overtaking.

───────────────

Elizabethan

Locks laugh and
Turn to silver.

───────────────

Imagine

Among the fields there was a small
wooden shed, once painted white. Inside it
a coat-hanger on a length of string,
wall to wall. A smell of cats.

───────────────

Ontological

is is short

Tuesday

Got up.
Stayed.
Went back.

Tuesday the second

Got up.
Made a list,
If needed,
To refer to.
Wasn't needed.
Went back.

I quit

Leaving a scatter of uncompleted projects
Rusting in the hilltop grass.

Thin pencil lines
Fading in a dummy book.

The party of children in wheelchairs at the planetarium
And their stately indifference.

―――――――――――

Hymn

Those who make humanity
The victims of society
Shall fade away.

―――――――――――

A repetition of Machado at Porth Gwrtheyrn

The soul creates its own shoreline.
Mountains of ash and lead,
Little arbours of spring.

―――――――――――

1. No one bears their torsion for ever
   It is worked out in the end
   In decades of patient study, in the stroke
   Of a fast car into a cliff-face.

2. And isn't meanwhile a glorious never
   To which the starry margins bend
   In decades of patient study, in the hope
   Of any old vehicle arriving at a meeting.

―――――――――――

Hope is flawed certainty:
We don't know what we already know.

―――――――――――

Oxford

The purpose of poetry is to unbewitch.

Current affairs

These vast spaces in our living
Vast spaces we have made in our living
Treated as normal –

Vast as to cover the world,
Treated as normal.

Social music

1.   A little shaking of the coffers
        Can revive a whole family.

2.   A little shaking of the coffins
        Can revive a whole nation.

The day's final balance, the grey hills
At night, the grass blades rubbing together
With a faint wavering hiss . . . .
Words breathed out in sleep.

Next I see her off at the station steer through the supermarket
Sit in a coffee bar in Leek return home drop a
Bottle of wine on the kitchen floor and spoon it through
A filter-paper to get rid of glass-power. What hell it would be
To view only the permanent.

GAAB: A short novel

1. Generous helpings.

2. Ambiguous polytextual concatenations.

3. Absolute certainty.

4. Bitter, betrayed old men.

Palindrome

The U.S. power
Stamped on Granada
Like an irritating bug.

A long novel

My body
Tricked me.

Are we cows, that they play us
Milking music in the supermarket?

Dead leaves in the emperor's garden,
Flame and ash in one, floating
On the cold stone ponds.

Derek Bailey's guitar

O entrails stretched across the negative rose!

———————————

Winter and spring are fighting it out:
aubretia in flower under pillows of snow.

———————————

About to begin

Blow on the leaf and it trembles in the clearing.
Let the bird go and it skims the river face.

———————————

Funny

Indo-European roots
Are a thing of the past.

———————————

Echo disposal problems

We are raising our prices, due to increased costs.
We are increasing the cost, due to raised prices.
The prices we raise, increase the cost.
The cost we increase, raises the prices,
As a result of which, we augment our charges.
The ices eyes us.

———————————

Why does the poem have to move out?
Why in the midst of the family at evening

does the poem have to look outside to the dark fields
the roads stretched over the hills, the unspeaking soldiers
passing by in lines?

———————————

(a)
If we could inhabit our own distances
We'd live faultlessly and never die.

(b)
If I could win myself back into time
by a perfect meaning I'd have
the entire slope into love:
Autumn water running down the fields,
reason to end.

———————————

Local studies

What a lovely morning for going shopping
out into the market place, windy day
sun comes out and goes in again
ambling round the stalls noticing
people I know here and there half noticing
people I'm not sure if I know or not
N.B., must stop hand-flapping it is
so theatrical it's almost television
N.B., must control vocal pitch better in
sudden hellos. And here's Emily pushing
Harriet who hasn't woken up properly yet. Christ,
look at the price labels on all this junk.

———————————

Return to earth

Old men planting cabbages,
Safe from all our hypotheses.

The Irish Voyages

i Sky blue and turquoise
   lichens on the stones
   and pockets of green-black fern
   in standing water.

ii A tiny bird, a stone-
    chat on the sea wall.
    A spill of hard
    resonant flakes
    down the side of the air.

iii Snow burns into the film of earth
     thrust by the wind into pockets
     and crevices of the promissory mass.

iv Cold: traces of fern
    on the electric kettle.

v The path is lost
   among wet stones.

vi What we called the doubts and
    cracks in the marriage were
    grains of fortune folded in
    our hands below the cliff.

    The sea takes
    up the light and
    casts it on the sand.

vii   Green ideograms on the white sand
      where horse and rider passed in the night.

viii Huddled together on a rock in the ocean
      for an actual belief, a lost
      point as we walk again the thin line
      of scattered debris to where we are.

ix   With no mention of anything modern, no
      doors in it. And no other light
      but the light of our countenances each to each
      no other light in the whole island.

x   A wrought-iron cross bearing a polished disc
      over a lump in the grass.

xi   Remember us, ragged
      petally ghosts,
      slips of flesh that
      crumple in the wind,
      outspeaking stone.

xii   I am tired of the new words
      for the old fears
      and the narrow escape.

No muscle tempts us from this house
With its music, coriander seeds,
Starlings talking double.

Do not pass GO

The state wants vegetables.

The state wants vegetables

Do not pass,
Go.

How to read poetry

I think the way to read poetry is with very bad eyesight,
screw up your eyes and peer at the words, which
fill the field, black quarry before you
and pale air all around.

So that you would only go to this trouble
with a telegram of some concern.

And secondly to believe everything you hear
for as long as you can.

I think of torchlight processions,
horsemen charging into the valley at night
then go to bed and dream about
being shouted at by schoolteachers.

We are worms in the company of statues.

It is better to be a worm in its own clarity
than a hero in a cloud of waste.

Narrow roads

The sloping wheatfields like animal hides
We'd stroke them with our eyebeams if the car
Behind weren't in such a flaming hurry.

———————————

Big question

Why do we do what we don't believe in
And then ruin everything in the attempt
To make ourselves believe in what we do?

———————————

Kojak

For after all
Death isn't the worst thing that can happen to you.

———————————

Spring arrives
      And the grass is fatter
Only the bites*
      Of reality matter.

*[*var.*: bytes]

———————————

After Du Bellay

Happy the man not constrained to conceal
The truth evident before his mind,
Whose freedom doesn't depend on power,
And people who mustn't be offended.

———————————

Only the decision at the crux of desire
      Makes route across a life
Travelling north, country sunlight
Sweeps across from left to right
Beautiful swift light taken at the logical hinge
      Of passion do not pass me by quite.

———————

Yaama

I am an old woman.
Help me to get across the river.

———————

Omnis populus

I go diving through the whorls and blasts of poetry
looking for your elegy.

———————

I wonder if that little restaurant is still there
that we had to ourselves, summer evenings in
the purple and ochre hills of southern France
quietly as the barman leaned on the bar
staring out of the window and the woman
in the kitchen smoked and the light faded
through the wisteria
into the wine.

And I wander as I wonder
and there is I suppose
something real somewhere
I might just wander towards
if it's still there.

———————

Count is all that size does

St Paul's still rides the city strong
beside the puny Natwest erection.

Here's to Willie Clancy

It seems quite simple to me
that you work at a useful trade
supplying wheat or paper or whatever
is needed and at other times
bash your forehead against the Zodiac.
Willie Clancy drowns out the pudding songs for ever.

And here's to Willie Boyce

This universe is not a product of chance.
Don't ask me how I know this,
I don't.
Doubt is my only certainty.
William Boyce turned his hand over, then up.

I didn't know Christopher Whelen was dead
(a plummy voice on the phone, almost trembling,
ordering books by Reznikoff and Prynne)
I never heard his music.

I thought I heard Jelly Roll Morton say

I'm some kind of a subordinate around these parts,
I don't deny my name.

I pick it up and shake it
like a sweet slaving chain.

Another poet begins an autobiography

Childe Hood rides again.

The history of the blues

1.
I went down to the station,
She wasn't there.

2.
There she was, begging
For a lousy dime.

3.
I missed my train.

Arcadelt / Bandol

A bottle of good wine in the bicycle basket
no lights, no policemen in the dark streets
working hard, reaching home with dignity.

"I found the wind more worthy and honorable
[than my love] and turned towards it."

For Harry Gilonis' Horace collection

I have made things of brass
That don't rhyme properly and won't last.

At night sense stands between
stars and earth features

Intimately knowable, so
don't delay, if

The road is too narrow
open the book,

Lost without fear.

Domestic pentameter crime-sheet

I wish the cat instead of chasing corks
would stop the snails from eating the Russian novels.

Polar sleep

When I die I shall unsee nothing but white darkness.

My failure

Cool air blowing in the window
and across the room

Yes yes yes but
you don't be what it is you
understand and love
you don't become that thing

Cool air blowing in the west window
and out of the east, lying here
wrapped in thick textures.

───────────────

Things survive because wanted

Not by how many
But how much.

───────────────

A stone house in the hills

The wind went round it like the weeds in a cemetery

───────────────

The moment at Buncrana

The two old men
on their way back from the gents
suddenly leaped into a two-step
and stood before their histories
joggling up and down
holding the rope that goes round the land's edge.

───────────────

Hermit's cave

A rest from forward foraging
and the presences burgeon, spread and surround,
the life of any,
the joy of real polyphony.

The & a

The view out over the roofs
and tree tops in sunlight

[hiatus here: a frightened arrivant,
an extended palatal fricative]

The mist wrapped into the tree-heads,
showing the course of the stream.

The new war poetry

Is nothing safe from our guilt?
Poor daffodils, we weep to see you
painted black.

Political Anxiety

All these books
all this music
how I miss the small
black and white cat.

After much travelling

There are cradles in the surface
of sufficient locality.

And language is kind, asks no victim –
small, still waves over coral tombs.

And in the night further and swifter, over
wall, over hill and dale, little baskets of sound.

ROYAL SIGNALS

From the war diary of Arthur Riley (1906-1983)[1]

---

[1] This work, written on 6th April 1984, is a collage and narration of phrases taken from the diary my father left behind of his experiences as a soldier (radio operator) in North Africa, Italy and Palestine 1943-1945. Any text outside this condition is italicised.

───────────

1943. Trucks to docks.
Five nights at Dumfries
Preston Manchester Kilmarnock
Donnotar Castle
Sailed down the Clyde
Church service in lounge
Left England
Rough Sea
No smoking on deck
Impromptu concert
During air-raid
Arrived Algiers
Marched to race-course (5 miles)
Entered the line.

═══════════

By road to Tunisia
(500 miles)

Through Atlas Mountains
(storks' nest on house roof)

Arrived at Ghardimoua
(concentration point)

───────────

Messerschmidt Valley
Longstop Hill
Germans within two miles
artillery
opened up
the whole Division

───────────

Very hot day
pestered by flies

Road muddy
Djebel Rhaouass

Dead lying everywhere

Reveille 4:30

Slept in olive grove

———————

Moved to Sousse
overhauled wireless sets

Lovely small bay,
clear water, white sand,
carpenters at work

Dysentery improved

Detailed to take charge of
A4 wireless station

Much shrapnel falling

———————

Established station on hill overlooking harbour
Fine view

Connecting set to teleprinter

Got through to the island

Apricots from the tree

Ceremony at ruined mosque
for healing

Got teleprinter working

"This is Radio Pantelaria calling"

Wilfred Brinkman came over
from 2nd Field Ambulance
talked of old times at Brandon

Opened up 12 set to take over link

Cleared ground of stones

Difficulty encountered changing aerials
for night frequency

Small white building on the shore
Moorish arches

Water in a bowl
in the sun

Truck over-turns returning
from Tunis
eight injured (Hiscox badly)

Hut across valley
celebrating all night –
drums and wailing

Quiet day, washing, mending, etc.

Melons grapes and tomatoes

Young Hiscox died at 3 a.m.
Buried today

Signal Office duty

Heard Soloman play,
Municipal Theatre Tunis
Lovely African night. Moths
flit across stage lights.

Spent morning quietly
sat with book
overlooking valley

Lecture on field hygiene

sang "Holy City"

"Just Us"
(piano drums sax and cello)
moths flit across stage lights
"L'Amour, Toujours l'Amour"

Hundreds of storks flying in V formation

Ascorbic acid tablets started

Kids fighting for biscuits

"Holy Father, Cheer our way"

Black clouds moving over the bay:
hundreds of birds like swarms of bees

Moved off at 3 a.m.
took 24 hrs. ration,
spam and cheese

Said goodbye to the General,
sailed into fog.

———

Stood out to sea all night

Opened listening watch

1944

———

Little sleep and cold

Dug pit in tent

High whistling overhead

Too noisy to sleep

Cold windy day

Flares up at night.

———

Quiet night. Lovely moon.
More bombers crossing to German lines
Saw one
break up in the air and
come down in flaming pieces

Going out towards front
on monitor set

Shell blew off tops
of roadside trees

We had to turn back

———————

Hectic night
shelling at close range then
single aircraft flying low
followed by more shelling
and so on, all night

Still alive but tired

Collins (B Sec.) killed

lack of sleep

large piece embedded in set

———————

Thank God for a quiet night

So far,
16 killed
34 wounded

Now checking frequencies
with wavemeter

Hundreds of crosses

Celebrated birthday Feb.22 in dug-out

tins of meatballs and spaghetti
"How Green Was My Valley"

Wireless silence in whole div.

Shelling close in the night. Tom Chambers
wounded. Fears he will lose leg.

12 planes dived on camp with AP bombs
killed Jock Baird and a MP

Tent peppered with shrapnel
then ammo dump went up
and half shells and shell cases dropped on us
had to keep under all morning

Checking frequencies now

Poor Jock, he was a good fellow

Repaired wavemeter

Lovely little robin
comes for crumbs every day

Earth tremors

Worst night yet, shells everywhere,
dropped in dozens. House hit,
guard killed. Ammo dump ablaze.
A1, A6, B10 hit. All wires down.

No reply

Raiders over Div. dropped APB
Burnt out 299 set and QM stores
Also part of G. office
Holes in my blankets

No reply. Why don't they reply?

———————

Called out in night to 2 Fld Artillery.
Passed Flyover Bridge and "Factory"
damaged tank and dead lying about

Slept in caves (rats)
nerves, couldn't sleep

Saw dome of St Peter's over hills

———————

Holy City
cheer our way

Bathed and washed clothes in stream
Slept in barn
Sets closed down

Refugees returning with cart-loads of furniture

———————

Tu dei saper ch'io
fui Conte Ugolino

Relay stuck, couldn't get i.m.
then engine failed.
Tried everything

Smoke screen
Mine field

Village ruined,
church blasted by shells,
used as stables

Loyals made push.
Moved into school-room

———————

Italians come to house for belongings
but go away crying "Niente"

(nothing)

Children beg food at cookhouse

Set up wireless room with receivers
and remote control keys

———————

The valleys looked lovely in the morning
with sun rising above the mountains
throwing shadows of trees across the river
and a slight haze of smoke rising
from the village below

═══════

Moonlight walk around Jerusalem
Old city

Labour govt. elected in Britain

Erected wire aerial
36' mast, f4410. 2170
heard explosions in the distance

Valley of Giants. Hill of Evil Council.
Field of the Shepherds. Garden Tomb.

Remote control
evil council
(nothing)
no reply

Set damaged or dead

and he was a good fellow
down in flaming pieces
why/when/where

Dugout cinema
stage lights flicker
sun on water
in a bowl
for healing

Open. Listen. Watch.

With a book
over the valley
shadows of trees

concentration
                      point
(impromptu concert tonight)
royal signals

(earth tremors)

distant
reply.

All I did, all I was –
death and life moving   under and over
me   against each other –

Concentrations   layered   in the distance
tapping out   continuous messages
garden / tomb of   distant home (of)
continual   Victory

Left at 1200 hrs.
Travelled all night
At El Kantara 0200
Passed through Egypt
Changed at Benah
Took Cairo train at Tanta
To Alex.
Handed in arms
1157 checked
Sailing WNW, passed Crete
Squally, saw Spain on port side
Arrived at Toulon
Disembarked and went to transit camp
Left by train, travelled all day
Passed through Paris at night
Demobbed.

Small Square Plots[1]

[1] Seven-line poems with seven syllables to a line, most of them over-written on British poems of the 1930s and 1940s. The authors of the original poems are acknowledged by their initials after the poem.

Now in these green and musty fields
the elusive flame day's hidden
meaning floats in the hedge and
flips past my ear like a ghost
saying love is wild and true
to the end, where is the end?
O come dripping to the 'phone.
      CWG

★ ★

Summer wipes the leaves a bright
glazier's green, tree standing in
a fuzz of cash, face value as
love contains an orange
on a wooden table: still
there nine years later hanging
cancelled debit on the air.
      DN

★ ★

Love that covers death like snow
under a blue sky at noon
pale minute yellow flower
veined through the frozen crust of
eyes days voices promises
of the Atlantic mind a
needle held in constant north.
      JFH

★ ★

Love wants to get in at him,
desperately, make him real
and lasting, a promise kept,
open access, a long peace

as the fruit of his process
but the chrysalis opened
and a hairy bear strolled out
                    RB

⁂

Lots of black cold. The thought that
made the world never thought it
would think so small and coldly
at the broad soldiers that bear
the breaking light on the black
flats, the free fens that hide what
we are, father out of night.
                    JCMcL

⁂

In the first idea of rest
was traffic and a distant
war, in the second idea
was a cushion called despair
finally the door opened
onto total loss without
the faintest sound in the air.
                    NM

⁂

Water breaks under the tree
to an ancestral rainbow
between reeds and written reeds
O love is restless there and
calls limb from limb and child from
home to a cold colourless
nothinged edge of air and sky.
                    TS

⁂

Coming back to the big blood
on the screen of days the towns
folding under themselves, what
separates weight and fortune?
The sky clears late behind trees
and lights come on the river,
lanterns fixed against sorrow.
      DC

   * *

I love slowly and stumble
through the spaces between words.
A bar opens in the voice
of no one I know, the long
river lights a way edged with
wisdom and my normal weight
prints warnings on the white sand.
      WSG

   * *

Day closes in a mad rush
to get the small letters right
comfort to the afflicted
soft words and luggage labels
meeting in the windy street
beautiful eyes fat commerce
what remains of a taxi.
      SC

   * *

A rich river with cliff-like
white hotels where steadfastly
I am hollowed against my
inventions in a slow tongue
remembering well, truly,

friendly with fear, run chatting
to a further fallen town.
                    AR

          * *

Bright architecture brighter
than its function and the world,
love's title-page, archipel-
ago in the sky a Roman nose
in a spread of faceless stars.
Then singing has a good room:
praise of persons, taste of tomb.
                    NM

          * *

No, have not gardened sorrow
but broadened the story home
of a love I held alone
against death's candle fences
skittled seven times to rest
in a garden of mornings
sonant with pillar-box caves.
                    TG

          * *

The grey hotels, the seven
syllables amassed in the
last resort. Thoughts are cradled
in loft rooms of cliff houses
to weight a beautiful lack,
a sea or carving, against
life provisioned into cloud.

          * *

More and Extra

(1) **More**[1]

Poems from *Reader / Lecture / Author*

Harecops

Grace and honour descend the hill, seeking
the human heart, brushing aside the wasps
and folding that knotted academy in clay hands . . .

Our front window looked out two miles over
pasture and woodland thick with the sheen of equity
that without a word edits thought against
greed and fantasy, pale emblems shelved
at the field edges, fading nightly into dream. We held
onto this like grim death, we sank our trust in
curtained arbours in a stone house and formed a child,
who mothered us through opening Sundays.

And two miles away was a great ridge, a dark
green mass strung with white stone walls,
at its highest point an ancestral grave, a circular
fate capsule of long stones. It was always there
though the light came and failed. At night the ridge
was a grey sleeper against the sky and white messages
flew into the front window, pierced the night and
focused the day, calling to the mind, calling
to the cusped heart, calling together
the kind forces that hunt us to death.

---

[1] Other poems from the trilogy and the Jack Yeats group will be found in *Passing Measures*, Carcanet Press 2000.

Macclesfield

Mislaid purpose coated with grime and stuck
in a nest of hill shoulders. Little red tractors
buzzed round the heads of the town
and the dark brick alcove was always ready,
you could sink yourself in it and belong
until you stank of oil. Question was:
did you care, did you want more than well being?
If you didn't you rested even as the evening sunlight
sat on the doorstep with its feet in the street
and you crawled between the slates and the cars
and kissed, blind to all except detail.
If you did, you worked the circuits crying O, Baby,
don't you want to go . . .

A provincial voice has total age or falls to scraps.
We took our purpose by the hand and led it
out of the factories and shops, into the nation.

Egbert Street

A name becomes hearted
and maintains life.
Somewhere between loss and gain, in that
narrow climate the flower succeeds
that grows now in the garden here,
a castle against relatives.

High Lane

I wandered the fields and woods,
waiting to be called back
into someone's life: the hand
on the shoulder or the teeth on the neck –
lay back and be taken or escape and kill.
I took a bus to the city centre.

Coming home late at night on the dark
walk from the station through the old mines
I glanced up at the hunting lodge on the horizon
and cast my affection forward against
all caution to that cage, believing
the most logical things on earth to be
the most sensual, tears in my eyes, knowing
the prize was not mine, well, such is
passion or day.

Sounds in the Nightly Air

The hunters' call across the valley –
us is what they're after
and can't fail either, in the end
we are theirs, and they take us.

Then the horn calls them back
to their silver folds and
the quarry rises
white against the green hill

And turns towards us, heraldic creature with
open arms, compact of ore and bone,
living and breathing creature I have
followed a whole life.

Then all our virtue stands in us,
hunted down to our core. Then there is
no further pursuit. Note also the perfection
when a face is distanced from its moment.

Michael Haslam

Congress of twins that
    lengthens the world
in a mournful music, send me
    back to the drawing board but
keep me for that fold until
    the diamonds fall
down the sky and we are
    sunk in generation.
Kit this pillow
    in a fabulous lace of spittle.

Regendered

You entered me and that
Point of you that means
Real and future has filled
The emptiness I held there
With seed. Now I trail
In the moon's path because
I am trapped in because and
There is a small light at my gut.

O That Singer

For Amédé Ardoin

You're fallen, the street at your throat.
Denial echoes under the palate as they
queue at the bank for promises, not

Believing a word. And you who believed
everything lie cast in a rail-side cot
blood-clot on the brain and a hawk came

And perched on the wire, beautiful thing,
preening its oily coat in red and grey
and beyond those unfolding wings

Was a cloud cumbered sky over
a measured plain where immeasurable pain, where
distant travellers greet the dawn

Eye to eye, hand to mouth
and never arrive. Never arrive
because the syntax is cut

Just where it opens where the
wooded hill cleaves in the wind, there
we offer pittance to your archive.

And we your friends, your very
loyal congregation set our hearts back
to the living light in the far shed for the hope

The day yet harbours, singing and playing.

From *Poems To Pictures By Jack B. Yeats*[1]

Music in the Train

No escape from a small country. An old man
Stands up in the train and plays his violin.
Ghosts pour out of it. Everyone nods, this
Is a music to die to, knowing what you are
Bound to and the train rattles on.
We pay a dream tithe to the ancestral hat
And head into the city looking for work.
I never asked to be out of this I was never in.
I never longed for another. Green hills out
Of the train window, touched by cloud,
Draw the very breath from my throat until
The only dying left is into this line.
Which is I suppose too a way, a rather
Circuitous way round the hill but a way
For all that of supposing, and launching
Your soul into the guess, that the work you do
When you arrive is good work, and time once
Properly located sets all things right.

[1] This set is also known as "Poems ending 'Time sets all things right'", which was found in an oratorio by Handel.

One Remains

I would like to die lying on a hillside
In the West of Ireland one summer evening
Crossing my legs and resting my right cheek
On my right palm with my latest companion
Standing beside me already wondering
How at that age to find a new friend. I
Like to think there are people I don't
Yet know who'll be willing to ease my way
Through that day's work. I shall gulp
The sunset I shall turn the slope on edge
And one stands there, he or she, asking me
If time sets all things right.

Music Night at the Old Slip Inn

Nothing less than exactitude: exactly
a 40 degree lowering of the eyelids
in respect of a national hope and the degree
of emancipation that might result, exactly
a high B-flat at the keystone of *The Last Rose*
lingering into a curtailed glissando
so delicate as to be unannotatable.

Sings his song, as he often has, a worker in the day.
They listen, and the moment stands still in its
becoming, where national is never enough, and
the spirit of the commune tunes the incus
to a greater reason. Becoming what? becoming history.

Yes, this also is history, this pub-singing, that constructs
a momentary refuge from hope, as from despair, a fragile place
(the exact sustaining of the final cadence) a place
of now, the very banner of the struggle. For here time sets
all things right. And the future, with luck, might set
a few things at any rate a good bit better than they were before.

On Through Silent Lands

To make of the heart a question mark
and forward artefact, a woven thing
held close and shedding purpose
on the ranges, slowly articulating
resistance, to the swellings of
oppression that crown human heads
with fear and disappointment. So the
isolated consonants, the shreds of colour
fleshing through the dark land –
the heart   the wish   the demand
a good life in an unjust society,
        a difficult thing.
What sign does the heart make
when the shadowed limbs falter?
        On through
silent lands, crossing creeks on
wooden footbridges, long tracks
winding over the mountains and
down great wooded valleys. Mud
on my coat, sky on my hands I go,
announced by lark on high as
hedgehog and hare watch from their
grassy stations. So the world has a chance.
        Through it
a traveller passes pressing a hat
to his chest as if the heart
needed protection from the rainy
convexities of the universe,
and from the wholeness that
burns a mind to stone. And from
the heart's own exclusivity.
And thus continues for weeks over
silent lands to the goal of speech
many troubles beyond, to the world's
rebirth in kindness, knowing
also that time (a known thing at
day's decline) sets (easily as river
to sea) all things (whatever's
wrong with them) right.

(2) Extra[1]

Poems Extra To *Reader / Lecture / Author*

Aigburth

Flower festivals, sewage
works, Chinese fish and

Chips. We
lived together, sharing

Our persons and
everything we were

For eight years.

---

[1] The extra poems do not affect the constitution of the original books.

Socialism

So many, bearing their own souls,
have truth and poetry at their edge
but prefer not to know it,
being focused on supply.
Later, when the world is better,
all these souls will remain
as unique scripts faithfully
recorded, after any of which
the world cannot be the same
but only a forward location.

Nicholas Moore (2)

I repeat, the heart, the,
the hart in the forest

The white one I would
pursue that forehead for

Ever and don't care how slowly
slow it comes closer and closer

Until the whole land is dressed
in the wholeness of a small animal,

A stoat maybe, a sandpiper, artful thing
that hunts / is hunted day

And night and day again until
that quiet end so fine and clear.

Poems Extra to *Snow has settled [...] bury me here*

Saint Louis' Island
First version

Again the bright label suspended in the sky
The new light burning in the old walls. Stone
Carves the water: neither an attraction nor
a privilege but a mercantile success – facta est,
A piece of work. Water encrusts the stone
With tokens of twinhood, symmetrical facets
Streaming in the river wind, a place that
Cannot sink to what it has become.

Baudelaire lived here then moved to outer hell. In
Memory of Berlioz I carry the heart monstrance
This bright morning through the wet streets and
Over a bridge into the stone crown. Aren't I also
The disqualified lover of vanishing states?
Aren't we all? Beams and signals hover and cross,
The wide eye of the street dweller calling to
The vertical fantasie of state O my lost brother!

Our forehead mansions, our genital smoke, skin
To skin we read our histories to the world
And fortune is what we dare to ask, not for the
Self, that sore, for the life. The vane
Skreaks in the wind tossed off the cathedral,
The shops open and tense like bees in amber
And fast in the new day where first and simple
Things are true, be grateful for every other.

Place Dauphine

I sit in the quiet place at ten p.m. A few people
playing boules among the trees by the amber lighting,
a dog or two being walked, a triangular square
of 17th Century housing with the river beyond it
and still capable of including a sewing shop for the locals.
I eat a sandwich greque with a beaker of red wine I carried down
from my room in Hôtel Henri IV which is OK but
you need to be at the front, I had a view of
drainpipe formations so I came down here
to the public place, exposed to passing trade
and the gentle wind that follows the river
rustling the leaves . . .

. . . guard our declaration, devolved
to a common purpose not any old common purpose but
a common purpose held in the indolent moment such as this.
Like a game, but not one, like a recognised good in
a casual emplacement, a moment of historical success. I love this
      place.
Baudelaire, come back from outer hell.

Notre-Dame
(envoi)

And then I thought of you.
I saw you in the fields
Of your own life it was
Truly the finest thing I
Ever saw precisely because
It wasn't mine or exactly
Yours but a future thing or wine,
An earth detail regained.

*Prose poems and pieces written
at the time of writing* Excavations

1. *The Songs*
When the dead awaken / and lament the condition of the living, the failure of language / that cannot say what we are or what we do // a sound in the streets, a smear on the rim of a glass / that which passes / carrying a bird cage through the streets of London looking for a removal van / because / a *non sequitur* is an unbearable thing / so follow it, follow that forward van as the old man said. The old man is laid gently in his grave, to join all the other old men / where are the songs we were promised?

Biting the tongues that feed them / rises over the fiery trees, and dies above this calm land / full of instruction.

2.
Write from henceforth, blessed are the dead and suddenly here they are, sitting under the pine trees playing cards, with musicians and dancers, with wine and food, ceramic tallies at their elbows. The moon reflected in the dark stream, the stars among plum blossom, tuning lutes and zithers these homiletic skeletons under a grey mound on a northern moor, *in cortesia* / setting us dreams of abundance to challenge everything we know, making poetry, the scoundrels.

---

3. From an abandoned alley (Peter Kennard)[1]

Hands claw at newsprint as newsprint claws at minds, force shoots from finger-ends. Whose hands? Whose minds? Where does disaffection become creation? What messages lie in the rubbish, the uncaring disjecta of the construction industry, the illegible numbers? The homeless in the streets, the sleeping-bag bed in the closed shop entrance and these are not fragments or waste but entire meanings at which the captains of the earth blink.

Hands and faces embedded in black surfaces / traces of people, faint outlines, dimly glowing quarters, profiles of wrist and shoulder, indistinct lettering... Buried in/ projected onto/ black tarpaulin banners rampant in decay. Traces of life in the tarry surface, movements of small winding shadows. And shall these one day speak or is the whole attempt to regenerate a society buried for ever in tarmac? The sleeping heads in the shop entrance, outside this turmoil. An anger which is not political.

Broken, failed, or unformed limbs, people become graphemes burned and printed into fired surfaces... Death floating on the sea as a flotilla of small lights. Little bells, like goat bells, tinkling through the night in the harbour of a small seaside town, floating eyes under closure. We wave the flags of poverty and obscurity behind the hill and fall nightly into the dream of belonging, anxiety and peace, death's musicians.

For death isn't the beginning or end of anything. Death is the central edge.

"How slow the wind [that blows these things away], how slow the sea [that calls to foreign shores], how late their [banners] feathers be." Q.E.D.

---

[1] From an exhibition at The Darkroom, Cambridge circa 1995. Ends with the quotation of a complete poem by Queen Emily Dickinson which was set touchingly by Howard Skempton.

4.

The wind and the rain / Will bring you back again / the forking paths between words, will lead you to the simple fact / the leeward strain, will close your pain . . .

Voilà donc des personnages bien hésitants sur ce qu'ils auraient dû faire dans l'histoire or to know the particular form of their courage

finally mocking any sum but the total

[— — — — — — —]

Goe from my windowe

5.
A step forward and the past clarifies. Geometry of the heartland, moon marks on the ridge, the river stepping down the vale... What we work to, lies here in the decided risk, the speech saying yes, on, yellow feather at the world focus as the chest empties into [song] bursts into [help]

Later is the silent river enclosed in night, the ferryman leans on the pole, later is sleepless dream. And why so far from the earth and its light, the beautiful earth? The black boat on the far marshes, no one knows why.

But that our story brings us here, to darkness and silence, broken by the slight push of water against the bank. And is completed, formed, a cup set on the shelf of a corner cupboard where the mouse p[r]ays at night. And says,

---

6.
The clue to the Neolithic star-farmers is song: they were mainly interested in singing. So all we know of them is their tombs.

The music that sets a valley in the mind. Up which we ramble, you and me (who are you?) if it is you, and not me, hand in hand… up the valley over the pass and down to the town. Towns are for us being buried in.

7.
The man in Jack Yeats' little water-colour (in the library at Sligo) singing his heart out in a village street in the middle of the night *O Sailor Rose of the Parting Seas /* stands still and sings, his mouth a round O in a fat face, the flower tossed in the wind releases its pieces one by one. His heart stands round him like a stone column.

Blind Lemon in some whorehouse, waiting, shuffling the epic phrases back and forth, two matches left, don't you leave me here. A cigarette, a column of smoke ascending.

"They had these emigration parties, when the son of the house was to go to America. And they lasted all night with the music and the dancing. And at the end, before it was dawn, the young man would pick up his sack and go, and they would all stand outside the house and watch him walking away. And the custom was that he would have a box of matches, and every now and then as he walked down the valley he would strike a match and throw it into the air. So they watched these little flares descending the valley until he went round the corner and there were no more. Probably they would not see him again."

The vinyl decays, the magnetised molecules on the tape coating shift back to the earth's fields, the laser marks on the CDs break into rust. The original voice heads out from the harbour past the metal man, rides the corrugated shining and sails for ever the arriving oceans.

MESSENGER STREET

Messenger Street

In memory of Douglas Oliver [1]

1.

In the harbour, in the island, in the Spanish seas...

In the hospital, on your death bed, which you suspected it might be,
you became again the beautiful boy your sister painted:
very thin, wide eyed, hood of grey hair, bright and inquisitive.
"It's as if," you said, "some god has decreed, this writing
has to stop." And as you explained about the cancer
I felt that Paris had turned its back on us, the Paris of wine and poets
and southern glow had thrown us out: we were cast into the world's
cold fields together, you and I, to wander away from all the love
we'd ever known. You wept, as you should. You had plans.

That night I crossed one of those steep, tiring footbridges over
the Canal St-Martin as a return to the uncaring mainland we
construct for survival, but with a new brooch close to my heart,
a cameo there of your new image, focusing the whole tenor
of your work on a helpless creature sinking into its cot
but bright of eye, and bearing that brightness on to a future
somewhere else, of which we know nothing, taking that
brightness away from us for ever, to some other purpose.

And the god who decreed this writing had to stop suddenly
whisked you away, over his back like a baby in a sack and strode
off beyond the outer suburbs into a vast outer darkness
in which a tiny light shone, a foetal worm gyrating
in impossible distance and this was you and the entire city
of your enterprise, a star-thought diagram, a rose in night's eye
as the months pass and small flames descend.

---

[1] Douglas Oliver died on Good Friday 2000 in Paris. *Messenger Street* quotes several times from his poetry, and also from songs sung by L'Orchestre National de Barbès, Coope Boyes and Simpson, Mahlithini Nezintombi Zomgqashiyo, and the Seventh Day Adventists Students' Association Chorale of Soweto.

Messages, which if we can reach them strip us of our privilege,
and leave us like old babies dazzled in the new day. They
lie around everywhere – in our hearts, in your books,
in the streets, in the very gutters of Paris. I pick one up
outside an Algerian cassette shop. It says,
"I must seek the goodness appropriate to my flawed life."
It says, "Thus would we pass from this earth and its toiling,
Only remembered for what we have done."

And what have we done, what is the best we have done?–
spoken the truth, sown the seed, which opens somewhere else,
where someone knows nothing of this name, this death, this
        darkness,
the future of our words and deeds a line of light on the horizon
towards which a heron flies, slowly, beating from the heart, slower
and slower. Stately bird, messenger bird, bird of good omen,
guide us to that gap in harm.

2

Douglas, listen to me, there are people in the world
with real hope, whose lives cannot be an incompletion.
I have seen them dancing
and singing, and sighing in the rain and going back
to where they live, in small flats above bars
somewhere beyond Gare du Nord. "When will Algeria
ever know peace?" they sing, and we who
"cannot know their secret joy" cannot answer.

With what fullness they enter the dance, is that the measure
of your death? Is it as far as that to a meeting place?
I don't know. I believe in the passionate transcript
that works the whole place, the whole city stirring
in its separate sleeps and winding into the dawn,
where after a long night an arm goes over
a neighbouring shoulder, and the hating folds into the love.
We are at our best when we reach that edge of stillness,
a line of light growing at the end of night

writing the ancestral store of kindness into the day
where we make perfect sense – shared,
and its failure, with the lost nations, don't we?

3

> We are at the source of the music, which will always,
> like water, return to where it once has been.

Yes, we are going home, we are ahead of us.
We have nothing in the end, which opens the door
of the first house we ever knew. Tears flow
down your face to feel your welcome there,
in the final closure of your enterprise to find
an access back, to where you started.

And the evangelists are singing, and dancing,
in the cavernous street. Our enterprises stop their ears,
we don't want to hear that, we know better.
We know nothing, and the heart sighs for such
plain hope, sighs for the one thing it can truly know:
we are in death with fields and purposes

Whose light spreads over corrupt spaces
and lightly kills them. We have a strength
in this clearance, deaths clearing death.
Mahlathini died too, and Rogie, I don't know
where any of them is now. Such lives
form a building site in the possible city

Where all the failure gathers and offers the world
something, something to engage with, a way
into a future, a thought that opens a door.
Listen to it, that distant singing, through
the mist on the hospital window, the gleam
in the glass that burns the heart out, the completion.

And we'll go together, arm in arm we'll go, in some
format of the world the world doesn't recognise,
and sit by the river and watch the cathedral
on the island and the light passing over the water
and sort out the whole bloody mess. Two old blokes
dead and alive, talking and silent, dreaming
of betterment, eyes full of common sky.

4.

Half-light of Dawn
A version of Baudelaire, Le crépuscule du matin.

The reveille sang out in the yards of the barracks,
And the morning wind blew on the street lamps.

It was that time when a swarm of harmful dreams
Makes the dusky youths twist and turn on their pillows
When, like a bleeding eye that throbs as it moves
The lamp makes a red stain on the daylight
When the soul, fretted and heavy under the weight of the body,
Mimics the hostility between lamp and light.
Like a face full of tears that the breezes wipe clean,
The air is full of the tremor of vanishing things
And men and women tired of language, and tired of love.

Here and there the house chimneys began to smoke,
The women of the town, their eyelids pale,
Their mouths open, slept their stupid sleep.
The homeless old women, dragging their thin cold breasts,
Blew on the embers and blew on their fingers
It was that time when, what with the cold and the dearth
The pains increase of women in labour.
Like a sob interrupted by a froth of blood
The far cry of the cockerel tore apart the misty air,
A sea of fogs washed the buildings
And people in pain in the depths of hospitals
Let out their final rattle in uneven hiccups.
The party-goers walked on home, wrecked by their efforts.

Dawn shivering in a green dress with pink roses
Advanced slowly towards the deserted Seine,
And dark Paris, rubbing its eyes,
Reached for its tools, old working man.

ALSTONEFIELD VI

The value of common emotions concerning
the passing of time. The counting of joys,
and changes of love, the sad persistence of the days
dragging our hearts out of us – more than the world,
more than the silence of work these things
convene our powers. Pain and promise move
the hand to sign the contract and we are again
engaged, reader, by a factor of the earth bowling
between us. Quickly on a warm day I walk up through
the smell of moist leaves to a sheltered summit.

And all the people in the land, as the clouds clear,
without priority, the fruit of work, all pain and
sorrows over. These are the ghosts in the white stone,
written in the strata: Go down, you blood red roses.
And all the work in the land, as the stars fade, doesn't
bear more result than a leaf reaching the ground, all
its joys a history. Such are the songs that surround us,
near and far to comforting me, shadows on the sea.
So with some sense of purpose on a thick morning I
pass by empty fields to a tree-crowned pinnacle.

Today there will be a wedding in the village. This
village, here, grey houses together like a cemetery.
And those other villages, full of people, busy working,
crowding the streets all day long moving, talking,
leading the beasts, bread ovens smoking in the yards,
everything out in the open. And other villages,
as the soldiers depart, human corpses in the street,
the houses heaps of smouldering ash, women some-
where behind the trees wailing. And the cuckoo in
all these places signalling its everlasting troth.

And the first swallows arrive, diving the ridges.
What is there beyond this knowledge but death
and fear, what is there to love in the cyclopaedias
of failure? The morning lark haunts the
falling air sweeter and gathers from its throat
the whole armory of the possible as a practical
course: known result, true outcome and
strong memory, when the gates open,
the creaking wooden gates without which
the gates of the mind will never open.

Those words first occurred to me (the last 20)
while listening to the group IZA in a smoke-filled
cellar underneath the Metropol in Cluj last May.
I wish you had been there, gentle observer
of these preparations, moving like gossamer
over the far fields. There is something sweetly
definitive in the grasshopper's lament that sinks
deeper into the possible world than any scriptural
displacement, any designated topping. They played
from midnight to three without stopping.

And the place rang and the rafters sang and those
who remembered the villages got up and danced
the dances they were born to. Something had survived.
Now back in the opaque world I clutch my lunch
and walk across the fields looking to left and right
for there are no paths here and security devices
have been purchased at high prices almost everywhere,
making us all feel rather insecure as we bear the burden
of the endless creation of markets from cradle to grave.
One day we'll work a way out of this costly safety

And attacks of peace-of-mind. But I got here, I walked
unobserved (fearing the shouts of angry farmers) over
the stone-boxed fields and climbed up Steep Low
and settled in a niche with my packages. And here I am.
Down there the village lies doggo, like a coin
in the earth, like an illegible stone, this village here.
And those others, full of life and death, full of
continuity, continue, somewhere beyond the line of hills,
beyond us and our parental ills, beyond guilt and favour,
the vast labouring populations work their wills.

The universities of the western world are full
of people in highly privileged positions making
great moan. While in those villages incessant toil
bursts out singing. Sadly too, of the bird winging
away for ever, the hopeful messenger, but held deep
in the throat wither all returns. There we have it,
there the maimed and the oppressed unite in a sleep
truer than the narrows of day. Indeed it is our habit
to sing at day's end, in the light we have preserved,
all the prizes the soul has ever deserved.

Sing, rise, turn, advance, offer, kiss, dance.
Do this for me, wedding villagers, before I go.
Spin your question on the stone hub: *When
shall we ever know peace?* In the passing
of how much time as bird after bird life after
life ruffles its body and leaves the ring and another
wedding is declared the musicians are again notified
their assistance is required in the attempt to chime
a future out of nothing. And we do: acts of hope out
of ruin, gather, turn, kiss, weep, shout, dance.

Our good songs have their melancholy ring
at the heart of procreation. *My rose, think well
of the beginning and the end, with whom you will cover
the world before your eyes. For it is not borrowed bread
which can be given back, neither is it unearned money
which can be spent, nor is it a hot pillow you can
turn over. You have found, rose, your life's partner,
winter blossom, fallen bud.* So they sing,
and dance it, in the dying villages not yet dead
to which increasingly my heart's dance is led.

Through the streets of Europe in the metal dawn is led.
Streets of northern Paris in the rain, under the railway
at Barbès selling fruits and spices crying *When will Algeria
ever know peace?* and working for a real future, which we
can never know, which is neither hope nor dream but
a movement, towards a space opening. And the whole
of the past is drawn into it. Then death cannot be
an incompletion – all the people in the land, all
pain and sorrows over, turn their heads to the east,
as if to the faint sound of maybe a wedding band.

The view from here is difficult, the village down there
somewhat round the corner, I catch the north edge.
The view towards Paris from Belleville one misty morning
small parks and white apartment blocks clouding
into the sky, the city in its opacity. You don't see it
but you know it's there. That vast sea of lights, throne
of promise, the surface of it. Douglas Oliver, with
a brandy and a cigar on the top floor of Tour Montparnasse,
or sitting on the slope of Montmartre at night, in pain,
his work silenced. Talking to the rubbish man.

The man from the east. The man from poverty. Not,
though, the only man. Poetry, impossible beast,
lifts on the wings of everyone, every lost alcoholic
camped in the central reservation of every roundabout
every forgotten island in creation, the heart of
every American soldier. Has no choice in this. Sets
the song in the air that forgets suffering completely
and turns in a momentary space of truth and safety
thinning at the edges, where the town opens out
and I sit on a hump viewing the vast hope drawn.

Unsettled because when I arrived in Alstonefield
I found the B&B had gone out of business, combination
of fatigue and Health & Safety regulations and all
the others in the region seemed to have gone "up market",
combination of greed and pastoral nostalgia. The water
still springs at the foot of the hill, the root still grips the stone,
those who can pay more inherit a rubber duck, and a star
scorches a path through the grass for a neighbour's sorrow.
I'd lost my rhythm, my recurrence, and ended up
at The Greyhound at Warslow.

And from there get in short time to the top of Ecton
in the late afternoon, in the dull light, and lean
on the summit post. The great hill scattered with
tumuli and mine-heaps. Such hopes for the world
as old socialists entertain belong here in bleakness
and raised distance. Where the devil's toe ripped
the earth the future angels sing. Lend them aid, anyone
with half a care, take your part in the silent chorus
spreading over the forsaken grass, spoil heaps, plastic
buckets and sheep shit. Gargle triumph to the age of debit.

I lean on the trig post. This really is my place, an
historical landscape completely unknown to the
heritage traders, a ridge top to deter all seekers
after loveliness, but beautiful. Crouch under
a thistle here and catch the verticality of fear.
Fall asleep on the downward slope and hear
the world cussing itself in stones and moss.
I sink into the wind, I squat on the tumulus, I
spy the stark stone-heaps on the far edge where
the last theatre closed. I am at least my own boss.

Rough pasture and mine mounds up here. Fallen
ground, crumbled stone, rusty barbed wire, red
yellow and blue plastic buckets among patches
of sheep shit, O God this earth is given us.
It is ours. And what are we to the godly book-keepers
but plastic buckets that hold something for a bit,
something nice, something nasty. Something that needs
to be disposed of. Shan't we each eventually
fan across the landscape like spreading lights
like lost kites in the wind of multiplying nights?

A strange sense of being observed. From the next hill,
from the small back window of a stone farmhouse half
a mile away, from the Christian despot himself. And
always that sound in the air, a groaning
that stretches from city to city across the land,
under the burthen of fear, for there is more profit
to be made from fear than anything else and easier.
It is our moan for the end of Old Europe, our
secret song, that gives delight and hurts not,
our unsellable souls vibrating in the overtones.

It was stronger on Morridge. I drove up there later,
at twilight, and stopped in the lay-by where
the phone box used to be (see *Tracks and Mineshafts*)
and looked out over miles of edge-land merging
into low Britain, as broadcast. Tiny sharp points
of light sprang up, gathering to a swollen
cluster down the vale, Leek. And that sound, more
than ever pressing down from the sky to tell us
we are run by those who gain. In a sense it is true
of poetry also, and paradisal homes. I think

it is time to stop, mid stanza mid flow mid
nettle-patch atop ugly hill, sensing the song wrapped
in the overtones of the common complaint,
a song of pure delight with no justification,
orchard colours sprung from the metal files. Posit
this as a human constant and stop, demanding nothing.
Hum it down the hill, leave it to the world.
Walk on the bones of the dead, start like a bird.

Notes to Alstonefield VI

I think this is a separate poem, but which retains its title because of its continuity from, and references to, *Alstonefield: a poem* [I–V] (Carcanet 2003). A number of things not noted here will be found in the notes to that book.

Stanza 5. IZA. A Romanian semi-professional group of musicians named after the valley of the Iza in Maramureș.

Stanza 7. Steep Low. A rise of ground in the fields near Pea Low (*Alstonefield* page 23 note), a rocky outcrop crowned with trees but sometimes interpreted as a burial mound, or as having been used as a ready-made one. The narrator remains at this spot for the rest of the poem.

Stanza 10. Italicised section quoted from a Transylvanian wedding song. See the third of *Four Transylvanian Songs* (p.206).

Stanza 15. Warslow. A village to the north-west of Alstonefield beyond the Manifold Valley on higher ground, thus off the edge of the Peak limestone dome, on gritstone.

Stanza 16. Ecton. See *Alstonefield* p.59 note. From here to stanza 19 the narrator revisits the site of *Alstonefield* pp.72-79, the "Sphinx" episode, remaining within sight of but at some distance from the mine ruins, and descends from the ridge in the opposite direction.

Stanza 20. Morridge. An edge representing the far (west) side of the gritstone moors from Warslow. The movement here is as if the choice of direction on page 25 of *Alstonefield* had been re-thought and a decision made to proceed westwards, towards the conurbation in the distance below.

PROSE PIECES AND PROSE POEMS

1992-2006

Manchester

Arthur White I remember you at the Experimental Theatre Club which was under a railway arch near Victoria Station, a makeshift auditorium and bar stinking of paint and damp and whoever else I remember there I remember you there.

Short dark pale man with slanting eyes because they said your mother was Chinese, soft spoken, sincere, neat, a good amateur actor who never pushed for a part and on the stage mysteriously became the most different thing, and the headmaster of an infant school who once said, the only time I ever saw you faintly angry, "Hit? How could I hit my children? I love my children."

Who lived alone in a bed-sitter in Didsbury which I once shared with you for a night because I missed my last train and said I'd walk, it wouldn't have been the first time I'd walked, ten miles in the night to my lodgement in Cheshire; we were all rather post-drunk at London Road Station as it was then called after a long evening in the bar and I was clearly a nuisance with my missed trains this schoolboy among us. And you said Oh come on you can't walk all that way I'll take you home and I shared your bed, I'm sorry I was nervous.

Arthur, I'm sorry, I was nervous and had indigestion in the morning because of all the green chârtreuses and wouldn't admit it but I'd like to say now that if ever I had been inclined to be homosexual it would have been by the example of your gentleness. Not you, I'm sorry about that, but your gentleness.

Well everyone said perhaps wrongly that you were homosexual as they said of many in that place the Experimental it was a refuge for theatrically-inclined question-marks, flamboyant mature women, failed professionals bearing up wonderfully, dedicated mechanicals, young women in various jobs soon to marry and indulging a last view of human variety, a few lost schoolboys and a man called Jim whose only ambition was to run the bar and did; and in those days inevitably, male homosexuals. But most of those had so cast themselves that the quality emanating from their presences was mainly some kind of outrageousness, and doubting schoolboys were scared; but yours was called gentleness. Quiet, thoughtful gentleness, and the kindness it implied.

Why anyway did I delve those warrens? I was working in Paulden's department store selling kitchen furniture and in the lunch hours and after work I roamed the labyrinth, north and east of Piccadilly and Market Street, the old commercial quarter of the city centre: every street every alley and ginnel every last corner I got to know it all by heart: narrow streets of office tenements, peeling and dirty façades, tall thick buildings, long sequences of name-plates beside half-frosted glass doors opening onto wooden staircases leading up to wooden office with long tables of typewriters, metal filing cabinets, light bulbs under metal shades, long windows hoping to catch some sky between the blocks . . . in one or some of which my father too had worked in his youth I didn't know which. And at street level the office doors alternated with smaller entrances to shops and basement establishments including a lot of lunch-time cafeterias and evening bars, gay bars most of them. I knew them all. I knew the names and directions of all the shops, I lunched in all the cafés in rotation, not seeking the best so much as determined to cover the field. I sat in the bars at opening time when it was quiet before the evening got going listening to the barman's inflections, wondering whether I'd go or stay. And the wider spaces too, the fruit market where anyone could go along at four o'clock any weekday and fill their baskets for nothing, and the larger avenues and squares full of peculiar shops, remote trades in chandlery, model engines, cork goods, pornography . . . You see, I had to face the fact that these things became, pretty well, people's lives. People far senior to me. Became what they lived for.

Plus in the middle of this zone Shude Hill book market which was a thing without pretension or deception: ten open-air stalls at a wide street-corner most of the books the same minimal price unsorted, books sold like vegetables, and clerks and shop workers came there every lunch time and built up libraries of real books for next to nothing: pocket editions, Everyman's Library, all those geological classics and Russian novels, with occasionally a 17th Century folio as an indulgence. 17th Century folios were what you bought when you did without the pudding section of lunch for a whole week. And the old bars in the Shambles, the half-timbered buildings round the Cathedral where lost schoolboys wondered what an oyster might do to them and ambled off to get a burger, that newer and safer thing, at the bus station cafeteria. And frothy coffee, and on to the Experimental...

Meanwhile there I was in the kitchen furniture department clutching a ticket to some university and every book I brought in, the sub-manager had read it. He'd read *Ulysses* which I bought from a porno shop near the Cathedral. He'd read *Point Counter Point*. He'd read *Childermass* – he didn't like it but he'd read it. He was a man with curly dark hair and a moustache, some degree Greek or Italian. He worked and he went home to his wife and children in a flat in Salford and he read; he never bought any books he used the public libraries. I followed him, I went to the one in St Peter's Square. It wasn't very big. They had the complete Yale edition of Gertrude Stein in plastic jackets and I read all of them. I didn't like them, but I read them. I think I would have caught him out eventually, the sub-manager in his dark grey overalls who seemed to do nothing but supervise the display and despatch of sink units and had read everything, but by the time I'd got a copy of *Finnegans Wake* to carry round with me it was too late, I was across the road in the lampshade department of Lewis's among such a bunch of lampshade fairies I was never to meet the likes again. Desire over there was genital carnival whoever you were. No one had read *Rupert and the Chinese Princess*. But the wages were higher. And behind Lewis's was a curved alleyway where the Manchester prostitutes offered themselves to passing custom six to ten each evening and one of them about the age of my mother would approach even a temporary lampshade salesman disguised schoolboy and say Want to come with me dear and have a good time? And to my excuse of poverty kindly directed me to some new girls round the corner who wouldn't be charging much, but that wasn't the point: I've been taken seriously, I must look like a citizen.

And back to the Experimental where, and in the other one too, the Green Room, a slightly less bohemian theatre club in another cellar but in the financial quarter where the streets were clean, there were poets too. Always there are poets. The city's poets, who used to meet in the big pub near Albert Square and some of whom even thought they constituted a movement in poetry, which had a name, which I don't remember. There was Allen Clark who should have been a poet he was dedicated enough to go on a solitary pilgrimage to Cornwall to visit Sidney Graham and I remember the two of us hunched over a table in a backstage alcove during a performance of *Huis Clos* with our ears close to a small portable radio with the volume turned very low in case it could be heard on stage, as the poet read *The Nightfishing*. I remember the tinny voice, strong and gentle, coming through the hiss and distraction, "Now within the dead of night and the dead of my life I hear my name called from far out . . ." Here poetry pierced its way through Manchester like the point of a knife. The three of us, me, Allen, Sidney, in a dark hushed corner, hoping not to disturb the rituals of enterprise, telling the rosaries of the earth.

Though it was a long time before that penny dropped. I carried it all over Manchester, among the dead. But as for Allen like so many later he shook his head, it was all too much, he didn't get round to writing the poems, or the poems weren't getting him anywhere, the weight was too much on him the teaching and the time and the future and he got rather thick around the waist (Arthur White pointed that out, there was something very strict about Arthur White) and moved to London where I found him in another amateur theatre in Ealing in 1965. I fell in love with his wife, who was small and dark and called Sue and chirruped like a canary. They parted later but not because of me, not for schoolboys. All I got after an extended campaign which included playing, very badly, the male lead opposite her in *The Playboy of the Western World* was one long kiss in a car park. For she was full of good humour and quite determined that this wretched, persistent child should get his kiss in the end – long too, and pressed tightly together, but it was he, the worrier, who left her later. I found her in Hove in 1968 working at a language school and about to be married again, to a man who smiled and said nothing but whose virtue she said, was that he was kind.

And Tim Conran, the successful poet whose success terrified me. I visited him most weeks in his Manchester talking poet's house in Victoria Park where it was all seriously getting somewhere, the real poet's study full of desk and books leading him steadily on into the university, on to the big publisher who later deserted him and eventually to America – a man whose income from poetry had already necessitated opening a bank account in Jersey to avoid tax. I was so impressed I could hardly keep my dinner down. I remember him as a very genial man who taught me a lot about Manchester and alcohol and he didn't know where I was going but he convinced me I should go on and go there anyway wherever it was. But his poeting as so often later disturbed his domestic arrangements, the bright young wife and two children, the failing crooked fruit tree in the back yard. When I left Manchester the whole edifice was beginning to fall apart.

Not, then, the flower of the city, whatever that was, more like the red leaves trodden into the pavement. But when you are a post-schoolboy it seems axiomatic, that is where your next learning is going to be or there is something there you have to get to know first. So you have a city before you, a new/old thing, with true elegance and lasting marks of virtue solidly there at what remains of its heart, and you head straight for the seedy backstreets like a wasp and try to ease yourself without damage into a crux of either/or. Believing too that your research discloses purposes defined by the exemplars who tolerate you, though it doesn't exactly, and the real fruit is rather in further margins of the attention which form unexpected memories. Streets bookmarkets kisses and quiet men. And you delve the labyrinth, to what end? If it is a labyrinth it should have a centre, the goal of all this seeking. And what is that core? What is the beating centre of all that diversion? There simply isn't. The notional centre evaporates into history and all that remains is a street map of its own making, but with signs of hope, signs of a kind not easily recovered in newness but which seem to cling to the air, and seem to inhabit the persistence and continuity of the entire habitation. Signs on the walls.

Which has since been totally demolished from one end to the other as if that could ever settle it. Leaving a nothing which says nothing to the questions that were asked, and which hang for ever in the northern air.

And when I say "demolished" I don't just mean a lot of dark brick buildings I also mean the socialistic ethic implied in the availability and circulation of unfacile artistic and intellectual substance of all kinds new and old to anybody with the guts to inquire, in an atmosphere where even an extremely demanding textuality could be at least considered and weighed against any direct information of the thinking body, by people who otherwise sold lampshades or shoes. With only a trace, in those days, of the attempted youthkult appropriation of culture into instinctual solipsism. A few coffee bars near Central Station.

It was demolished everywhere. The library became a supermarket. I hesitate to say that the heart of the city was demolished.

And what were the questions that were asked? They were questions of equality but not of freedom. You found your freedom as best you could in the liberality of an equilibrium. The hope of the question lay precisely in equality and the way that, contrary to the fears of all the artistic autocrats whose books you carried under your arm, equality understood as an absolute potential actually opened the world to personal realisation, whereas freedom merely annulled generosity.

But occasionally for some reason or other I'd find myself in inner Salford. Salford is rarely mentioned even now. It is Manchester's "twin city" on the other side of the River Irwell and almost as big but clearly off-centre. Once I was sent on an errand from kitchen furniture for two urgently needed taps. Other times there was a pause and I wandered over one of the bridges. Or I might even have gone on purpose. I was never there for long. I don't know what's happened to Salford since, I don't greatly want to. Occasionally I was the other side of the river in a different country, I was in stone-clad streets and squares among low brick cottages pubs and small factories with squat chimney stacks and all the behind-the-scenes production and distribution slums of bright commerce. It seemed that here life had a single purpose, but a purpose which meant nothing because the purpose was the furtherance of itself and life was for the continuation of living lives, with taps and formica and corn-flakes delivery schedules. I shuddered with horror. We were living there like stones, like stones of the street. We were death. I don't mean the people they were well enough I'm sure, I mean the race, the human race. It was flat on its back in the puddles with a tray of shoelaces. I couldn't believe it, I still don't. If I went there now I expect I'd see mainly second and third generation immigrants in much the same scenario, I don't think much would have changed. There might be generous cultural margins but we focused our working time on smallnesses, our equality flattened to a mean materiality and it was impossible to breathe, stifled by a dense hopelessness that no amount of geniality could mask. I shall never agree to it, whatever it is. I make a terrible mess of the days, but I never agreed to Salford. In the end there were conflicts between that broad liberality of the thriving city where any worker might have access to the fullest reach, and that which made the city thrive, which stripped the worker of everything but abject ambition, and grew fat on his/her heart-consuming worry until the whole country is steered on fear. The burrowing had to stop. In the end it didn't matter how any bunch of seekers wrapped themselves in the fabric of the town, it was going to go on as an illusory thriving running into the ground. The creative focus lay out of sight.

The last I saw was Arthur White. I bumped into him twenty years later in the Opera House at Buxton during the interval of Cavalli's *Jason and the Argonauts*. An opera enthusiast, somewhat disturbed by the focused stasis of early Baroque – he liked it but you sensed he was longing to get back to his Puccini – but riding everything on the same old dolphin of gentle, sincere, goodwill. And not alone, a silent friend, and very much the same person very much he I slept with in 1958 and so generous in his asking that in the interval spent telling him what I was "doing now" I learned nothing of him at all. But there he was, the same and apparently well and good-bye again, Arthur. On the paper here, I give you a long, long kiss.

Alstonefield

The light fills the ground. It comes welling up at evening to the wheat tips, grass sheen, the whole pelage iridescent, slanting and falling to resonant quick streams. And when you look into the distance you see tiers of pale rock breaking cover, tier upon tier like the layers of a crown rising to the horizon where they break like waves into a sky darker than the ground. It sports the badge of earth, the whole cross of moment.

So it is difficult to believe here, the way its quality fills all the possible space, that what happened in the 1992 General Election in Britain was real. That the lie extends to the centre of the pie, and most people will agree to any bloody war on promise of a small increase in income immediately cancelled. But when you know a place really well you have no illusions; its fall is spread on it.

The Inn is cheap and wholesome, and that is the end. There is no third section, no answering stanza. In our own time we go there, take our meal and wine, pay for it and stroll around among the fields in the twilight. The old barn stands in the long grass, the church clutches its ancient carved heart, the land pitches on all sides into steep valleys full of quick silver. The evening is held on its brooch, and increasingly full of suspended trust.

Gropina

The stars clustered in the valley base. And what do you learn of humanity? Nothing (humanitas non solo stet) and what do you learn of the world?

Leopardi

The world shrinks as the population increases, and the known inflates, and the hiss when the sun goes down into the sea is no longer heard. Whose mind was tensed between star and sea, within fierce longing and knowable truth. Whose despair created a typeface. Whose darkness is born into our best dreams, where zero is an aperture of hope.

Gropina

Live in tedium, of course, sheltered by dream. Sheltered from earth figures and their brilliant despair, making the trade routes glitter at night.

The Locality

Quiet at night, rows of long narrow strip gardens. 1880s railway expansion: streets of workers' cottages built parallel to the railway line with long narrow gardens at the back for market gardening. Some of them still grow vegetables, old men tending rows of cabbages, carrots, potatoes, onions, with glass houses and woodsheds. Dark and quiet at night, no one moves, no one there. Three old men in a row, three brick cottages, three long strips of tilled soil, empty in the winter. No fences – only newcomers build fences and walls; one row stops where another starts. The old men sit in their rooms in the evening: three lit windows in a row, watching television. But one had a passion for roses and turned half his strip to a brilliant display every summer, with orchard trees at the back; the next stuck to plain veg., but the third cultivated the company of small birds by clearing the space in front of the window and putting out water and bread on the ground and the shed roofs. None of them married, who knows why – married men having a reputation for not living exactly as they might wish or growing vegetables only as instructed. They would joke about this, and the women would have stayed at home and cooked and cleaned the house . . . So no children, and children leave anyway, leave you alone towards the end of your life doing what you want or always have done, rather more slowly and with some difficulty, and problems with newcomers, mainly because of cats. Young families: every time an old man dies the house is stripped and renovated and a young couple moves in, proud of newness, gender conscious, world thinking . . . need more space: extend the houses further back, need more bathrooms, need more loft windows, put fences round the strip gardens, fill them with rabbit hutches, flower beds, broken furniture – and cats. Some have as many as six cats and can't seem to stop acquiring them. And the cats don't have enough territorial space in the fenced strip and wander all over the vegetable gardens tearing the ground up to shit in holes, frightening the birds away and killing some of them. And the cats eat the slug pellets carefully set in rings round the cabbages. The slug pellets send the cats into paroxysms of drunkenness and vomiting. The old men are accused of poisoning cats and the cats' lib office up the road is informed; there are unneighbourly questions. The old men go to bed early and nothing happens in the dark gardens but a faint ground-level rustling, perhaps a hedgehog, a faint erratic movement of winter leaves and in the air the low continuum of the city like a distant waterfall

Sant' Alvise

Sant'Alvise has canals on two sides, and sea on the other two, and there is only one bridge. The bridge delivers you straight into the campo in front of the church. Stone paved square with the church on two sides of it, plain Gothic brick façade late 14th Century with central oculi and doorway, lightly stone-trimmed, and above the door a 15th Century Tuscan statue under a small stone porch. To the right the facade of a large convent which occupies the entire south-east corner of the island. Long pink-faced buildings overlooking two canals with rows of green shuttered windows. The nuns never come out, and in the church have their own screened gallery or "hanging choir" above the west end, gained directly from the convent. Every evening at eight the windows and shutters of the convent are closed and all the lights switched off. Inside the church, on the right of the west door, are eight little 15th Century tempera paintings by a pupil of Lazzaro Bastiani. Ruskin thought they were early Carpaccios.

It's always quiet, especially after dark. You can continue through the little campo behind the church through a small area of 19th Century blocks standing on pavements, or turn left and walk along the fundamenta and back – plenty of people live here but there are no shops or restaurants and people do not seem to be outside much. In the evening the occasional person taking a dog for a walk, a small group arriving or departing through one of the doorways.

This poised, domestic place, part of but also absent from, the great city, as if watching it. Like a sleeping watchman, in the simplest form of the livery.

Which is pink to deep red with brown patches and soft grey stone trimmings. There is not that sharp confrontation of dazzling white marble and black shadow that Stokes speaks of, there hardly is anywhere – that's not what it's about, do you think this place was made by feeding our necessary continua to the ecstasy of death's final cut in supreme artistic solos? The moulded

Gothic window frames stand in the enormous red brick walls of the Frari, stone and brick bonded together, clasping each other's hands. Stone and brick not contraries, but complementaries. The space before them is full of articulated light.

Through the passages behind the church and a little further round two corners lands you in a small campo with some grass on the edge of the sea. So already you're on the other side of the island, at the Sant'Alvise vaporetto stop – standard yellow waiting-room bobbing up and down on the sea at the end of a short gangway. In the evening quite dimly lit, and a couple of street lamps on the edge of the sea. Black sea, and every fifteen minutes one of the little water-buses sails along and curves into the stop, ties up, slides back the rail, takes on or off maybe a person or two, maybe not, and sweeps away, curving out to sea with a tilt and a flourish. On a clear day you can see the Dolomites from here. Or at night watch the planes coming in to land at Marco Polo, lights flashing lower and lower over the sea then dropping into the nest.

You can walk back from here to the busy area of San Leonardo in ten minutes. Or get any vaporetto that comes along, and they come along all night, and go wherever it's going, it doesn't matter – left round the end of the island and down the Cannaregio to the Grand Canal, or right along the straight shore to Fundamente Nuove and round the whole eastern end of the city, and if you stay on it long enough this will bring you round in a big circle by the Grand Canal and Cannaregio and back home again. Or you might get one which is going out across the lagoon to the northern islands, Murano and Burano.

Standing at the side of the almost empty vaporetto at midnight as it coasts the cemetery island, holding the rail, slightly rocking, the black sea slides past, warm air blows across the face, and the city lights one way and the sea lights over beyond and all the darkness gathered onto the invisible cypresses in front. Death, what other darkness is there worth a thought? And that great office, that grassless, treeless, headquarters – over there over the water, calmly wedded to the centre of its own life, its gold ring.

St. Alban's

An island whose edge is defined by the concept: too far for children to go and play. The south and western limits were busy main roads just a hundred yards away. Where the ground was open the island extended much further.

Areas of unused ground, the bigger ones usually called "wrecks".[1] Houses round them, wooden garden fences and brick walls. Footpaths across them forming short cuts. Bumpy, uneven ground with tall grass, nettles, bindweed and the biggest of them, Woodbank Wreck, covered in rose bay willow herb which in summer turned to a field of purple flowers and in the autumn released masses of white down which floated through all the streets. A mile away you'd find white down floating through the streets. Wrecks, where you went to play, to cover the ground, to hide, and to see the sky, to mount a kite, in the war the barrage balloons hovering over the town.

A lot of disuse because of the war. Tennis courts behind the houses merging back into field grass. A concrete roller abandoned in a dip of ground, which you couldn't move. Areas which seemed like little stream hollows but had no stream in the bottom and were really humps of grassed-over landfill. Occasionally a wooden hut, someone's pigeon-coop, or a big one which was the headquarters and wood-store of the local builders, now back from the army and ready to start building more houses.

A gap between old houses on the main road with a low wall in front of it and a notice, "Site for Branch Library". Behind the notice, rough grass and small trees, ruined outbuildings at the back, with an area by the garden fences of the next road where

---

[1] Roy Fisher has suggested that what I call "wrecks" were properly "recs." short for "recreation grounds", reverted to waste ground due to war-time disuse. I think this is correct, but we, the children, definitely knew and thought of them as "wrecks" and none of those mentioned had signs of any decayed facilities (the tennis courts were elsewhere). After the 1940s they were without exception built on.

nothing much grew, green and black undertree spaces scattered with excrement. A footpath across, short cut into a back alley, saved three minutes off the walk to the infants' school.

And a big, empty, untended, "park": grounds of a grimy stone hall called Woodbank, with an old reservoir, copses, two ponds covered in duckweed. Ponds with reputations, where someone (named) had once drowned, thin fences and shrubs round them. Labyrinthine tunnels in rhododendron thickets near the hall. A long wood cut through the old estate where the ground swept down to the valley meadows of the River Mersey, which was the north and eastern limit.

There, far from home, creeping along the side of the river. Standing on the edge of the weir, the water covered in foam. Following it round, walking on beds of old overgrown sluices and flood lakes. A stream bursting from double doors in a culvert. Further back, orange sandstone cliffs over the river with a set of steps carved over their shoulder, down which we crawled, backwards, reaching a ledge a foot wide on the edge of the water here slow and black, which led to a small riverside cave in the sandstone, six feet deep with at the back a rusted iron bar ending in a ring emerging from the solid rock. Nobody ever found out why.

Dirt roads, "unadopted", most of the year full of puddles which could be channelled into each other, embanked in mud walls, walked over noisily on ice. You could play French cricket or piggy-in-the-middle in the middle of the road uninterrupted all afternoon. Smell of earth and wood, like a Transylvanian village.

Wrecks, tips, areas not yet built on, traffic not yet running. Sloping cliffs of ground-fill, which could be colonised, dug into on the shoulder, platforms made, dens, earth and clods mounted round them and sometimes a kind of roof with sticks, look-out stations. From which we looked out and saw the distant houses or the tall garden fence just below us, wood creosoted black.

A rectangular acre of ground off a dirt road, not yet built on, dark Victorian houses on two sides of it, shallow pools where leeches and newts lived. The newts, some of them magnificent kings, were brought home in jam jars but always escaped. The leeches were viewed with incomprehension and left alone. Green-black blobs pulsing through the water, with invisible teeth.

We called this island Offerton, or Little Moor, or Woodbank, or Saint Alban's. It seemed entirely sufficient, standing on the edge of the little cliff on the unbuilt side of Park Lane, dirt road leading to the stone gateposts, looking out over half a mile of Woodbank Wreck, it seemed there would always be exciting excursions beyond the island, always returning. The ground banked up against the long estate wall on the right, looking northwards towards Manchester, looking forward to sailing off again across the lagoons of industrial haze and red sunsets to a series of small, distant, stations into further life. From here, as if the island core would last for ever.

On the western limit a boy of ten ran out of a house straight under the wheels of a heavy goods vehicle and was squashed to death. Bright red blood ran down to the edge of the road and turned to flow along the gutter and fall into a grid. The butcher came out of his shop and scattered sawdust on it. Shoppers stood around, helpless and defeated, mentioning his name, which they all knew. Brick cottages with their front doors opening straight onto the pavement, and no more stone than a doorstep, and a plain lintel to each door and window. The body was in one of them, under cloth, the lorry was stopped by the roadside. Death strolled the western limit. I knew he was pleased with his work. I held my mother's hand.

3rd April 2003

Tonight I listened to Berlioz' *La mort d'Ophélie* in memory of Ric Caddel, who died the day before yesterday. I listened to all three recordings I've got: choir and piano, choir and orchestra, solo and orchestra. And I thought that the little four-note motif that Berlioz devised, repeated again and again at the top of the texture, representing Ophelia's song as she . . . You remember, she floats downstream singing, supported by her billowing robes. I thought this motif was very like the one Nino Rota supplied for the trumpet in *La Strada*, though I haven't seen the film for many years. If I remember rightly, it was all she could play, the little, pathetic, impaired girl who died. She was dumped in some seaside town and someone looked after her for a while and she spent most of her time sitting outside playing this motif over and over again, and then she just died, of nothing, she just floated away because she couldn't stand the fact of cruelty, its being in the world. And he thought he heard it, didn't he, in the distance after she'd gone, he was drunk and knocking over oil cans in rage and ended up sitting on the shore at night sobbing, and that little motif on the trumpet was . . . not heard, but it was there. Her robes became heavy, steeped in water, and that which had supported her dragged her under.

I hung these two deaths on the wall under a Hungarian icon of the Angel of the Annunciation, in memory of Ric Caddel, who died two days ago. But knew all about death, long before that. How it makes us see with our hearing. And our hearts remain: "magnificent pointers / out of galaxies."

What People Have

In the afternoon, walking across one of the town's big grassy open spaces, we overtook a tall old man slowly pushing a supermarket trolley along the metalled path. He was bent steeply over it, his head twisted to the side, his step uneven and painful, and in a voice like a drainpipe he was saying two words over and over again in a continual drone, which at first I heard as French, "M'assister, m'assister, m'assister..." But what he was saying was, "My sister, my sister, my sister, my sister, my sister, my sister..."

27/12/2004, 11p.m. Kemp Town, top floor, a strong wind. The potted plants on the balcony vibrating in front of the white wall. Solid cloud sweeping across the moon.

Offer this to the distant ones, the perfect, the children's children: Take it, keep it. You need it, this fault, this being right here. The fan heater makes a fluttering noise. Flights of elsewhere that sustain us, wired into now. Was it one of you that hung up the paper fish?

28/12/2004, 11p.m. Kemp Town, top floor, no wind at all. The big glass panel and the white wall beyond seen through an image of the room. Low cloud layer erases the lights on the hill.

What can you do with this, merciless ones, the powers to be? You don't need it, leave it alone. Haydn at Guantánamo, turn it off. You don't hear the wave break, structuralists. The wave breaks anyway, across the earth. One of the survivors constructs a paper hope, red green and yellow, with two enormous eyes.

Last Bus to Argos

The turning point at which the first lights appear, not yet really needed. "Lighting-up time", used to be stated daily in the local newspapers, at which the traffic was expected to switch its lights on, though it wasn't dark, but was beginning to be, was on the edge. A solemn theatre of points of light, across the surface of the earth. Gate lights of a small factory in the middle of the vast dark green countryside. Particular locations identified out of a subsuming spread. Orange and blue or violet lights appearing among trees in a small-town square, glimpsed between houses. Occasional house window lights on the side of a dark mountain, or in long stretches of olive fields. It is the end of the terrestrial day, however much it may be prolonged in the indoor theatre, which as we continue gets longer and longer into the night, and starts later and later in the morning because we need to buy the light rather than have it given. On over green expanses, mountain sides in the distance merging into the sky. Flames leaping from an old oil drum in the corner of a factory yard, consuming the day's residue.

Palladian Abstract

According to me, the two Palladian churches on the Giudecca, San Giorgio Maggiore and the Redentore, have their west ends facing north. They point towards Venice as their place of origin. Through the now glass doors of the Redentore you can see it across the sea, a rectangle of blues and red, in movement with sea surface and passing boats, in a white and grey page. The direction of meditational movement in both churches is from that distant richness of origin to a small, bare, monochrome simplicity. Everything is pared away once you pass the high altar. Worldly and intellectual wealth is focused, diminished, and eventually eliminated in the passage across the sea, into the colourless grandeur of the façade, through the assertion of sheer mass in the nave . . . It is like a cave, it is like going through a cavern narrowing to an alcove, to reach the fearful scratchings at the furthest end of a palaeolithic cave. Beyond the high altar, in the chancel, two simple arcs cut the white stucco of the ceiling in the shape of a mandorla, an empty pod, in the thin excluding light of dawn. All the richness accumulated during the sun's daily journey is stripped away in a reverse movement back to the break of day. In San Giorgio the alcove mouldings become single lines. After the high altar the denticulation which runs right through the church as a high course, is no longer pendiculate, weighing downwards, but projects horizontally, weightless. A soft retreat of time to the edge of a closure as a swelling and subsiding magnificence, by no means a tunnelling but opening outwards, really, to a stripped earth. The simple clean and adequate hospital bed in which we cease to refer.

And begin to be a point of reference. A point to be born(e in mind). In the shape of an eye, a pod, a seed, the result of two semicircular arcs set in different planes.

Lorand[1]

Smooth mountain sides in the desert, resembling the slopes and curves of the human body, ("flank" . . . "haunch") bearing the sheen of human skin   The desert at dawn, scattered small lights: facets of fractured rock, grains of sand, insects . . . small lights moving as if very far away   the intimate presence of the Earth, breathing in your ear

A point of light in the desert, the colour of the desert   and at night a point of darkness, a black dot   the pupil of the eye   like a small flame changing colour   yellow to red   and at dawn blue and white with streaks of rust   the need to protect this very small flame, to house it in a globe of thin glass, with access to air: a scientific instrument   revealing what we are: the eye staring into the eye and seeing landscapes there   of great beauty unmarketable   the star over the Judean desert its light entering a shrine

And someone arrives   from very far away   from nowhere and from absence   exactly on time   the doors swing on their hinges   "a sort of luminous saturation" enters the room from the direction of the sea   and the world is articulated in its immediacy, by exactly what the hand touches when it reaches out: a cup, a knife, a shoulder, a fossil ammonite, "the great leaf of day" as it turns   two people

[1] A "mémoire poétique" as he called it, of the writings of the French poet Lorand Gaspar.

towards each other   "an undelayable hunger
for birth"   sea and blood, light and
shadow, hinged onto each other and opening,
in Patmos.

The house by the sea.   Someone lights a
match, before dawn   a fisherman sets out in
his small boat on the striated meniscus of deep
blue ink   an unexpected dawn wind sweeps
over the stone fields   raising a cloud of pale
dust   in which a voice speaks   "The thunder"
(the fire, the strife, the Logos) "directs all
things"   the Strife that coheres . . .   ". . . but
I can hear the song", the Love trying to heal
the Strife   and the eye of the small fish in the
mountain stream   always searching

Through mud, through histories of war
("having suddenly lost our ancestors") seeking
a page of ideograms   a new ikonostasis of
peace and virtú   diving into the sea,
looking up at the bird in the tree   an ancient
pine in a Chinese ink drawing, an embroidery
of discrete signs   under which the wearied
travellers sits, and listens to the stream   the
chatter of small birds in a small white courtyard
in Sidi-bou-Said, two long-haired Siamese cats
half-asleep   the slow forgetting of histories
and noticing what comes from further away,
beyond the sea, over the mountains, beyond
memory   not a deity but a substance, to be
inhabited   two fiddlers and a cimbalom in a
distant village in the hills, Gyergyóalfalu   the
sound carried in the breeze over the plain   a
dance in which everyone joins   n/um – the
power to heal.

Derek Bailey's Funeral

The plucked string resounds but the finger no longer plucks it.

I was in Paris when Derek Bailey died, on Christmas Day 2005.

A falling away of sound, a hardening, a silence – the final victory of matter, its return to inertia. The notes rise into upper partials and fade.

In Paris it snowed lightly, a fine powdery snow that was scattered here and there on the ground among all those light-coloured buildings, all that pale stone, white to white, on grey.

A harmony of overtones resulting from a discord of fundamentals.

In Barcelona the parakeets squawk in the umbrella pines in the parks, each for as long as it is able and then passes the duty on to another. A tall thin man of 75 and his younger wife pass beneath the squawking pine trees regularly, day after day, each time moving more slowly, moving less and less, like a vibrating string no longer renewed.

No recording can deliver us from the new silence, nothing replaces the music which isn't going to be made. Somebody somewhere has got to make it.

Carpathian Pieces

1999-2004

The Lay-by Refreshments Hut

Between Oradea and the border, no more than fifteen kilometres, we were stopped three times by Romanian police and told we had been found "speeding" in a "built-up area". One of these might have had some justification, the other two were among wide empty fields with no building of any kind in sight beyond a dilapidated byre. Under the circumstances we would not be prosecuted but fined on the spot, but this was later put more succinctly as "You hand over 50,000 for me and my mate". We handed over. This kind of thing when you're not used to it provokes suppressed anger, internal speech-making etc., which is tiring, made worse by the attempt to drive everywhere at the Romanian town speed limit while all other traffic shoots past you, because of course they pick out foreign cars for this exercise and the rest don't need to worry.

But we were able to sail through the border post and carry on towards Budapest. This meant crossing the Great Hungarian Plain, the Puzsta, one of the biggest completely flat areas in Europe outside Russia. But for diversions round one or two towns the road goes almost dead straight for 250 kilometres among uniform fields. The Puzta is still thought of as a vast prairie of open grassland with a lot of water, like the Camargue, with its cowboys and its horses and its shadoof wells eerily marking the skyline. But most of that is now in a theme park; the whole zone has been drained and made productive: endless, endless dull fields with linear plantations here and there, the most energising thing in sight the occasional pair of storks.

And quite a lot of heavy goods transport on the road, all of it going somewhat slower, or somewhat faster, than us. After 200 kilometres of this I felt like death. I wasn't exhausted I just desperately needed a difference, a hill or an accident or a kangaroo bouncing across the road or a group of angels descending with a chalice. I felt I couldn't go on, my brain was in revolt. The road avoided towns and offered none of its own catering; I was even beginning to think that a Hungarian Fortes would be quite welcome. And in this condition I found myself able to pull into a lay-by and stop, where there was a small wooden hut with open front counter, and some hand-painted signs, offering "refreshments".

I stopped beyond it and walked back to this redemption. The road was highly raised and fields of crops lay below it, a small settlement beyond them with a path discernible leading from the back of the Refreshments Hut between fields to the village. There was also a sign pointing downhill behind the hut to the "toilet". A young man wearing glasses stood behind the counter.

He could have been any kind of person. This hut might be his entire career and prospect, he might own it or he might be employed by some canny villager, he might be a student earning his fees. He knew some English, indeed his numbers were fluent. I bought a salami sandwich, mineral water, a piece of cake and quite unnecessarily, a rather big pack of sweet wafers. I would have bought anything. I wanted to tell this young man that his stall was wonderful, that the service he provided was invaluable, that it was clean and well appointed and easily negotiated by foreigners, that it was well stocked with the right things, that it was timely and perfectly judged. And I told him all this as best I could in the only language available: purchase.

Sunday Evening in Botiza

A warm Sunday evening in Botiza after a scorching hot day, and of course many people are out in the streets and open spaces of the village. Lights on in the bar, and the food shop next door which is also a bar, and the hardware shop next to that, which is also a bar. Quite a lot of men sitting and standing outside the row of three shops, at tables or on the edge of the sidewalk talking animatedly with occasionally a murmur of song. Groups of men and women through the village, sitting on benches or walls or standing, some with bottles some not. Half a kilometre up the main street a big bar used by young people with music coming from it, crowded inside and spilling out into the street. People are not, as in some villages, very much dressed up for display on Sunday evening – they mostly seem to be as they usually are, as they would be any other warm evening, but more of them. Elderly people sitting on their verandas in narrow side streets, alone or in groups, speaking to each other and to passers-by. Nobody working: not washing clothes in the river, not carrying burdens or tools, not guiding animals. Children here and there, in groups or pairs, walking around, running, standing, talking, playing games. The young girls have the unique privilege of walking round in pairs in affectionate physical contact: arm in arm, arms over shoulders and round waists. People who meet kiss each other on either cheek. These things are coded. The priest's wife with her small dog on a lead, has crossed the big open space in front of the bars with the stream and bridge at the other side of it, and is standing talking to another woman, also in a dress and so probably also of the class designated "intellectuals" – teacher, doctor, etc. The dog sits obediently on the earth. There is a cart parked across from the bar with two horses waiting, occasionally rubbing their necks together. As the evening progresses light from the bars gradually seems to increase.

A six-wheeled heavy goods vehicle from the quarries or mines higher up the valley passes at a moderate speed along the main street, past the row of bars and on down the village towards the main road. It covers everyone: men, women, old, young, children, babies, peasants, workers, gypsies, intellectuals, drinkers, loafers, talkers, singers, dogs, horses . . . in a thick cloud of grey dust.

"I am a Poet"
i.m. Barry MacSweeney

We were staying in Szárhegy, near Gheorgheni, in the house of a retired Hungarian couple who constantly fussed round us in the most charming manner, totally possessed by the instincts of "peasant hospitality" although they lived in a big village now only partly agrarian. He was a retired construction superintendent, waiting for a state pension which was already three years late in arriving. In their kitchen/living room we were given a splendid dinner with a delicious demi-sec rosé made by the man himself, and then went out to stroll the streets of the village.

The street they lived in: long, straight, unmetalled but evenly surfaced, other streets off it at right angles, a grid. The houses all one-storey, moderately substantial in the standard pattern, standing in their own kitchen-gardens with orchard trees and wells, wooden fencing round them. All individually decorated, many even with drain-pipe corners bearing flower-like constructs of the same metal – and equal: all more or less equal to each other.

We turned at the end of their street into a slightly more important road leading towards the centre. We passed on the right one of those long low buildings we've seen in many places, probably relics of communism, which people seem to have difficulty finding a use for. A row of rather high small windows in a dirty white wall along the street, doors at each end, and no signs of use in the windows. But the last window with its door, someone had been able to make into a bar: the white wall-paint newer and brighter for the last ten metres, lights on, a couple of tables with chairs on the sidewalk outside it, a few men sitting there. It had been a hot day and was still warm in the dimmed light of a pale cloudless sky.

As we passed by a man stood up from the tables, crossed the road and came up to us. He was small, about forty, with a drooping moustache, thick ear-length dark hair, and above all two big sorrowful eyes under bushy eyebrows. He took hold of my hand and continued to hold it gently, saying nothing at first, perhaps deciding which language to use. Then, still holding my hand sandwiched between his two but without any pressure, he said in Romanian, "I am a poet. But my brain has been destroyed by alcohol." And his big mournful eyes gazed into mine while we nodded sympathetically and waited for whatever came next. He stayed thus a little longer, then without any further business he let go of my hand and returned to the bar across the road.

The BBC at Lunca Ilvei

A BBC camera team with a well-known presenter had been sent to Transylvania to make a programme to be shown on Hallowe'en, with emphasis on the creepy: ghosts, vampires, wolves etc. Why else should they come? What else could possibly interest anyone about Transylvania? They turned up at Lunca Ilvei and were housed in some kind of hostel down the village, the four of them. They knew what they wanted.

They wanted a night campfire meeting, immediately. They had no spare time, it must be tonight. It was arranged, in the fields behind the stables. A quite large bonfire was got together during the afternoon and word went round to about twenty villagers, and us. The two village musicians were also needed – accordion and fiddle. These were smallholders who played locally as a hobby or for slight extra income, and their repertoire was a selection of pieces from all over the country. The accordionist was quite good, though his *forte* was small flutes; the fiddler was rather ineffective, but the accordion carried most of the music.

As it got dark the fire was lit and the cast was assembled on a grassy bank in front of it, sitting on the ground or standing, in a small arc, which by careful camera control could be held to represent a whole circle of rustics around the fire. The ground was damp and quite muddy, and a strip of plastic had been put there for sitting on, hopefully not evident on screen. In the centre of the arc sat the presenter, an Irishman, interviewing Julian, illuminated by the glow of the fire. The BBC had supplied two crates of beer for the crowd, which were appreciated, and mainly because of this, I think, the general atmosphere was happy, in spite of the artificiality of the situation and the discomforts involved.

Because unless you got into the direct shine of the fire it was rather cold and there was an occasional slight swirl of rainfall. Also sitting on the plastic on the ground was not too easy and there was a tendency to slide slowly downhill. But still the general atmosphere was happy; people chatted, drank the beer from the bottles, and the musicians played, with some people singing among themselves to some of the tunes, and the interview proceeded.

Julian is a good raconteur. Stories about bears and wolves. About finding a bear up your apple-tree in the morning. How wolves would come down to the village from the mountains in the winter and he'd sometimes hear the howling at night. The presenter was obviously not very bright and things went best when Julian himself led the talk on from one thing to another, under the presiding spirit of the zuica[1] he was consuming. There was also interplay with the villagers, jokes aside in Romanian which might have said anything for what the BBC knew but which the company thought were very funny. In particular there was among us an adolescent girl, a member of Julian's casual house staff, who was apparently very sensitive on the subject of "boys", to whom Julian would throw suggestive remarks which got squealing responses from her and the whole thing went down very well with the crowd.

The trouble was, whatever was said and done, the presenter or the producer immediately said, "Do/say that again", including all the casual banter in Romanian. Everything had to be repeated, a second or third time for a better camera angle or sound take. Of course it was never as good the second time, and very much less entertaining for the villagers, and these doublings made the whole thing drag on. And there were other troubles, such as inane questions which Julian had to cope with and try to make the chat interesting again. And the cameraman had his own problems. He was evidently very good at his job, working dextrously with a hand-held camera, but had been eating unwisely since he entered the country and was suffering from a fairly severe attack of "the shits". So the proceedings were interrupted again and again by him handing his camera to the nearest BBC-person ("Hold this a minute will you") and dashing off into the darkness, directed loudly by Julian to a group of trees at the back of the field.

[1] A strong home-made fruit brandy

It took quite a long time. Finally the BBC crew looked at one another and said, "That's it, we've got enough." They got themselves together, and moved out, escorted back to their waiting car and driver, quite thankfully I think because the cameraman wasn't the only one who was ill and they all looked tired, and they had to get up next morning for a horse-and-trap ride through the forest to Castle Dracula, a renamed 1980s ski hotel about 20 kilometres away.

But the musicians played on, and everyone stayed. And they did some very popular numbers which most people joined in on, and the dancing started. It was colder and darker and there was fairly definite gentle rain, which nobody paid any attention to. The fire was a big heap of glowing embers now and in front of it they danced in the mud, for about an hour. Twirling couple dances, in mud. It was the best part of the evening, by a long way.

Two Beggars

a) *Little girl with the blue dress on.*

A young girl in a blue and white dress. The first we noticed was not so much her appearance, but that something was tugging hard at the third finger of Beryl's left hand in the attempt to remove the ring on it. We looked, and there was a young girl in a blue and white dress walking alongside us earnestly and openly trying to steal the ring, without so much as a good-day. She must have been observing us as we walked slowly along the main street of Vişeu and planned a grab and run, but the ring was tight. When we perceived this and stopped her she showed mainly resentment at being interrupted, and far from running away, she stood in front of us and moved instantly from thief mode to beggar, but in terms of demand rather than request. She was about twelve, had dark skin and frizzy hair and a sharp, active face. The dress was so much a little-girl's dress, it was a cheap little-girl's dress with rudimentary flounces and frills, it wasn't gypsy[1] wear and she seemed quite alien to it. She spoke loudly, incessantly and stared defiantly. She wasn't taking No for an answer. The coins we gave her, admittedly amounting to very little more than nil, were unacceptable and she flung them into the street. We didn't get a word she said but it hardly mattered. She was saying "Don't give me that worthless shit". The inclination to give her more was countered by her own aggression and tenacity. A somewhat higher sum was accepted but it didn't stop her performance and we made for the hotel. She clung to us relentlessly, and as we passed through the hotel's door she reached the pitch of striking Beryl in the back with her clenched fists and even then didn't give up but followed us down the corridor until intercepted and ejected by the staff. The rest of the time we were in the town we didn't see her again, but every move into the streets or round a

---

[1] In all my writings about Transylvania I have, like many other writers, chosen always to use the word "gypsy" rather than "Rom". This is partly because it translates the locally used "ţigan / cigány" as "Rom" doesn't, but mainly because there are several classes of gypsy, and in this society "Rom" designates the lowest, which nobody wants to be called.

corner was accompanied by a wary eye open for a pretty blue and white dress. Never mind pickpockets, brigands, drunks, muggers . . . what we're worried about is a little girl in a blue and white dress.

It left a nasty taste. We should have said something, anything – "Listen, yes, we will give money to poor children who ask for it, but not if they behave like this . . ." Anything, to establish some contact, something to break through that quite monstrous and self-defeating act.

And yet she never stopped smiling. Through the whole thing, through all that onslaught and pursuit, there was a constant smile on her lips to the very end, and there was a proud calm in the smile somewhere behind the histrionics. For it was also a game, which she can hardly have expected to win, and quite possibly she went on her way when ejected from the hotel feeling that a small adventure of her devising had been accomplished, even an impersonal revenge achieved. I can't be sure of that, and perhaps she simply didn't know what to do.

She certainly had a great deal to learn about begging, but something completely different from begging was in possession of her. Her demand was for claimed dues, as a right, with all the contempt. I guessed that this pride would either eventually get her out of her condition onto some eminence, or produce a complete disaster within four years.

b) *Little old child lady.*

A year and half later, in Sparti in Greece, we encountered her contrary. We were taking coffee in a donut bar on the main square, which seemed about the only place active enough to provide a view of local humanity. It was plastic and tiles, with some dozen consumers seated in its corridor-like space alongside the serving counter. A gypsy girl was begging round the tables. I think she was gypsy though she didn't have the physical features, but the headscarf, shawl and long skirt, all in gentle green and brown colours, suggested it. She was probably a small 14, and wore sandals on a cold day. What was startling was the elegance, the blown kiss. For she said little, and that quietly, and inclined her oval, charming, face and gently held out a cupped hand, not very far out, and got something, always, and then retreated with an animated smile and blew a kiss. Everyone, however little they gave, got the blown kiss – and graciously, with a little toss of the hand, tilt of the head and the warm smile. If it was acting it was superb acting, there was no question of failing to respond to it. But it wasn't acting; it may have been a routine but it was meant. It wasn't so much that she was grateful, but that she liked people.

After she'd done the rounds of the tables there was no dropping of a pose, no sudden hardness. The face remained calm, her movements smooth and gentle, she remained the little old child lady in the shawl as she sat at a table, counted her money and then went to order a sandwich from the counter. They knew her, and I'm sure she got some discount or something extra, probably without asking for it. She sat down again to eat, perfectly self-contained, not looking back at any of her benefactors, a task achieved.

I never saw anyone refuse a beggar in Greece, and the amounts they gave made us feel ashamed. We gave a few of the smallest coins and they gave notes. In a bar in Athens we saw two young working women in a bar give a small boy ten euros each, without really being importuned at all. He just stood by their table holding a small accordion which he never seemed to use and they asked him about himself and got out their wallets. I wanted to call the little child-lady back and give her more, but she'd finished for now and quietly slipped out of the bar.

Is it a question of how to beg? or of virtue rewarded? or of both – a skill so finely tuned it can only derive from a quality of the heart? It wasn't demeaning and it wasn't insidious. What it meant was that she knew that the world was basically a good place, and what you just gave her proved it again. As for the future, you just prayed it would be kind.

WALKING PIECES

2004-2005

17th November 2002, Youlgrave

Sunday. There is an open shop, and welcoming person: "It's a friendly village . . ." Bread, tomatoes, and some very fine Stilton. Set off westwards though the village. The singing chapel, standing beside the road like a stone transistor radio, emanating harmony. Muddy path over mine mounds towards Long Rake, and over the top pastures. One remaining tumulus, Calling Low, hidden in the woods to the right. A small pond of liquid mud and cow dung completely filling a gateway. Stonewall mountaineering. Sloping grass fields perilously slippery in places. The steps down into Cales Dale, taken very carefully. A jay below, gliding up the dale, perfect speed neither early nor late. Like the Methodists, in perfect time. Down to Lathkill, over the spring and left upstream to the head cave. Eat an apple. People passing by always stop here, whether it's lunch time or not, and gaze at a volume of water issuing from a cave mouth in the valley side, suspending thought of good and bad or what comes next, happy to be reminded that the earth continues. Death is kind. Strong flow today, though it hasn't rained. A man with a small dog's head peering out of his rucksack. Walk back downstream, quietly singing improvised hymns to myself, because you should sing, and people used to sing. Death is suspect, and needs persuading. Tough walking on stones, the path gets involved with the river. Left boot lets in water on front edge of upper. The day thou gavest. Though it's hardly started yet. Into the private sector, barbed wire, walking by permission, otherwise similar. River overtakes on the right. Walking much easier now, so that vacant hollows form in the mind. What shall I do with them? Leave the valley and climb up to Over Haddon, last seen circa 1956 and gone dead: no pub, no shop, half the houses Peak-Parked so they look like public toilets. That's wealth. Return to the valley, on down lower Lathkill. Vacant hollows throbbing. A few people about. Companionship of the old and the very young, travelling across all those years in an instant, a no-time which is unconstructable. Trout jumping waterfall: the energy thrust and impetus needed to stay where you are. Hollows contracting. A grey wagtail at Conksbury Bridge. Road back to Youlgrave slow in the rain. Big notice for

Countryside Alliance stuck on a barn: "It's worth fighting for." Vaguely disgruntled privilege parading as militancy. Left and right, blame disguised as praise. But love creates no outsiders. TRUE LOVE CREATES NO OUTSIDERS! I don't know anything about death but that's what it is about love. So I found something to do with one of the brain bubbles. A receptacle. The truth calling low over the hilltops. And onto the High Street again, still raining, seeking oatcakes (the floppy kind). No oatcakes! Oatcakes finished: EEC regulations concerning the bleaching of flour. That's progress. Dinner alone at the house and the day ends. Village night silence, with the river muttering below and a few owls in its trees, but still a silence, a specific silence. Maniac hammering on the door at 6 a.m. and screaming about a parked car.

Alpine Zones: The Reward

Why do we come here, hurt ourselves, strain body and mind to the edge of endurance? The valley of a thousand streams. The impossibility of the place. A thousand streams up there, a thousand quagmires down here.

The thin waterfalls high up the slopes, misty, incessant, aged presences. The streams trailing down the valley sides as raggedy white lines, which when you get up to them are substantial torrents, crossed with great difficulty, leaping with yells onto tufts and wet rocks. The Chinese aspect is half way to the sky.

The river divided into three above Peyregrand on the valley floor, rattling over the stones, waded with ease but icy cold. Three times we stand on the edge and fling as hard as we can two pairs of boots, and a large rolled umbrella, over to the other side.

Many azalea bushes with small, rose-like, deep red flowers, all over the hillsides among the rocks and boulders.

Big patches of dog's-tooth violet mixed in with the grasses. I zip open the tent flap in the morning and find my nose touching one.

Occasional wild tulips, all closed, red-yellow streaks emerging from the ends of stems. Then suddenly three of them beside the path wide open: big six-pointed yellow stars.

Three kinds of gentian, which Lawrence wrote as "burning dark blue / giving off blue darkness" – the miniature, the normal, and the attenuated or "trumpet gentian" (is this official terminology?) At wild heights, deep blue flames among wiry grass.

Hellebore in great quantity, mostly not yet in flower, lush clusters of ridged leaves close to water.

If you attempt to sit on the hillside the wiry sharp-pointed brown grass penetrates your clothing and pricks you.

The snow-melt late this year. High up, big patches of snow still remaining, perilous uncertainties across the paths, upper surfaces crusted and pitted, sometimes concealing quite big streams, which you can hear passing under the snow.

Insofar as there are paths in the uppermost zones – small piles of stones on the tops of boulders.

Mountain pastures crowded with orchids, mostly purple but also yellow, and orchid-like flowers, among which an unidentified sort of miniature turret of red cabbage.

Crowds of hyacinth, and yellow daffodils, and the "narcissus-flowered anemone", and the smaller daffodil, "the poet's narcissus", white with slight yellow trumpet. Dozens of them at a time.

Alpine zones in late spring. Snow-melt, swollen streams, a million small flowers. Small everything: small butterflies, small moths, small ants. Small junipers. Wire grass like needles. Small birds, a few. Small ripples over the whole surface of the lake, deep green. Cirrus on deep blue.

How the flower species seem to accommodate themselves to the available terrain, as if not in competition. A richness not dependent on an elsewhere. The result no doubt of a great deal of diplomacy.

An iridescent turquoise beetle minding its business on a grass stalk. A minute moth exactly the appearance of a petal of speedwell. Pastel blue with white border.

But where are the birds? This is lammergaier land, where are they? And the vultures and the eagles? In two weeks all we get one raven at Tristaina and a raptor disappearing into a fir tree near Siguer. And small greyish fluffy things darting over the snow so fast you can't see them, emitting a noise like a telephone ringing.

A little thunder as a bank of snow detaches itself and falls into the lake.

Why is the lake called "Tristaina"?

However high up you get, through whatever steep declivities and rocky paths of agonising demand across and over massive geological barriers from shelf to shelf many hundreds of metres into the sky – the animals and their herders have been there before you, the dung on the ground, this year's or last.

And no flies. Instead: dung-beetles, small black shiny creatures in clusters, crawling around and flying, which never seek to interfere with you.

The continuous sound of falling water, wherever you go. Wherever you sleep.

It hurts the body to move. It hurts the mind to fail. It hurts the spirit to contemplate the economic and social condition of the Principality of Andorra.

Never an easeful step. Where to put the foot, always a problem to be solved, even downhill at some speed. Rock edges and water routes share the pavement. A mediaeval muleteers' track, in some parts supported by quite massive masonry built up against the wall of cliff or canyon, in other parts vanished without trace, dispersed into bog and bilberry pits, leaving you to cross a torrent as best you can.

The main road becomes the illicit route. From France to Spain by the Port de Siguer through Andorra, trod no doubt by merchant caravans, troubadours, wide ranging shepherds, and later by Cathars, a precious book held under the arm, the only copy...

and Cathar persecutors. A muleteers' route, a smugglers' route, an escape route for Jews and resistance during the German occupation, a group of which intercepted at Siguer village in 1943 and executed by shooting against a wall on the north edge of the village. There is a plaque.

Finally lakes. Mountain-top lakes nested in cirques, great cliffs plunging into them or maybe one side melting out into pasture. Clear or choked, but the only flat things within 20 kilometres. Bent lakes following the valley curve, or placid almost square lakes in the tops surrounded by snowy crests. The surface covered in small ripples, the water absolutely clear, very cold, with, when drunk, the metallic taste of recently melted snow. And water falling from these lakes over shallow ledges to trail down the valleys accumulating more and more substance from side streams . . . Always the sound of falling water wherever you go and whatever you do, wake or sleep or walk or toil, stand still or lie down to rest, alongside the sound of falling water.

And at night the star dome, magnified and clarified in the great cut above the valley sides. All the rustling water on the deep grey sloping earth, and up there they stand silent on pure black distance a crowd, a crown, a vast donation, the reward.

Why we come here. Two people walking down a small road in the Pyrenees in gentle rain under a large red and white striped umbrella from Asda as the daylight dims. No other reason. A song-like reason.

How to Get to Ágios Pantaleímon at Boularií

When you reach a modern Church, the Dormition, you're in the upper village though there aren't any houses to be seen, just a few stone towers higher up the hill. Walk on up the road, which crosses a stream, and look for a small rock outcrop to the left before the white wall of a smallholding. This is the beginning of an old mule track which continues beside the wall, then meets another track from the right and goes on in the same direction beyond the village, following the contour of the hillside, running between low stone walls. It's a little used track and stones from the walls have fallen into it making a difficult floor for the foot in many places, and vegetation has sprung up from the dry brown earth, most of it bearing points and spikes: small thorn bushes and ilex, various thistles with purple or yellow flowers, bramble-like plants that trap your legs and can trip you up and scratch you at the same time. You need quite heavy trousers but some of those spikes are so strong they will get through denim, particularly those of a pretty yellow thistle bearing a round daisy-like flower with a cross of four long points behind its head, on the end of a bending stem. There is also a small spiked seed-pod which has a habit of getting inside shoes and a thunderbolt-like feature of conjoined stalks which detaches itself from one of these plants and by a band of barbed Velcro-like surface fastens itself persistently to any textile, especially exposed areas of socks, and is difficult to pull off. These enemies are not dense on the path but you are rarely free of them. After 500m there is a small ruined church on the right made of big stones, which a collapsed roof makes it impossible to enter.

Here the route departs from the track which just seems to disappear and you are among old disused olive terraces. The only path through them consists of that made by the very few people who make their way to St Pantaleímon, so you watch carefully for worn ground surface and gaps in vegetation, continuing ahead but slightly to the left of the terrace courses. That is, keep straight ahead but tend left. Go straight forwards, but think left, or allow left to happen as by a slight gravitation. Watch particularly for the blaze of deep red soil each time the route cuts to the next terrace down, only a metre or so deep. Look ahead, but thinking right, for the glimpse of a small roof of long stones among the trees about 100m away, and when you see it tend slightly to the left of its direction and you should enter a small enclosure of very old olives among white rocks, and then advance towards the church.

It looks like an old stone hovel, sheep shelter, cowshed, with the slight but tell-tale projection of the apses at the east end with their own fanning slab roof. The whole thing is no more than 20m long with a roof over half of it. You can get in by where the north door used to be, a gap in the wall with a wooden pallet placed across it held in place by an upright stone slab (replace these when you leave), into the west end which has collapsed completely and is open to the sky. But the east end is still intact, like a cave in a series of three arches before you, with the ruined iconostasis wall coming in from both sides at the last arch to mark off the curved space at the end. The wall surfaces from the first arch on still bear frescoes, at first fragmentarily among damage but increasingly intact as you get to the east end. They have been dated by an inscription to the ninth Century.

Keep on walking. The two great martyrs stare out at you from the two apse alcoves with both hands raised, *orant*, their heads crushed into the arching roofs of their spaces. Pantaleímon to the north, Nicetas to the south, old-blood red robes, ochre for skin, white marks for ornament, what survives as blue-grey-to-brown for hair and bodice. Pantaleímon, a doctor of Nicomedia who after being Christianised stopped charging for his services, martyred c.300. Relics of his blood kept at Constantinople, Ravello, and Madrid miraculously liquefy on his feast day. Nicetas, bishop of Remeciana east of the Danube in what is now Romania: a Goth, believed by some to be the author of the Te Deum, killed c370 in the persecutions of Athamarian. These completely dominate the figuration, there is no space for the Virgin between them and she is set centrally in a lumpy band above their heads. On the north sanctuary wall is an odd picture of the bathing of the holy infant, the body immersed in a kind of grey horse-shoe and the haloed head of a man of about 50 looking rather indignant above it. This is opposite the baptism on the south wall, and these are what remain of a cycle of the life of Christ which would have filled the church walls. Keep on walking. Push through the thistles and briars. On the south wall outside the sanctuary is a remarkably well preserved figure of St Cyriaca, another Nicomedian martyr, one of six maidens who died at the stake in 307. But a different martyrdom, a later fresco in a different style, with a more sophisticated regular patterning of ornamentation superimposed on the robes. A smooth, a forgotten death, and a large wasps' nest above where the wall meets the roof. Go back to the east end. Broad red lines on white, blue brown and black patches filling the outlines, rough-cut jewels of paint. Two martyrs. Look straight at them but think round them. Push past the enemies, the attractiveness, the foreignness, the remoteness. Look at the big serious faces, the raised hands, denying access. Speaking of fanaticism and a kind of love, speaking of focus and the self tunnelled into its purpose, to the point of suicession. Where the self ends itself, for the sake of a future, an unknowable. And what survives, in the profession of doctor, the history of concern, from these far distant lives, what seeds of extreme distance still stick to us. The two big pairs of eyes looking back at you, wide open, full of death. This is what you came here for.

# Poems from Abroad

2000-2005

Vertigo

Moving out of the tree border into the top grasslands.
This is the earth, and this is us here very close to it,
watching the great valley below, everything clinging to the ground
small black ants on my arm butterflies in pairs in the grass
I'm working on a statement of political hatred black
flies gentle breeze clinging to the hillside carrying
a few birds down below, shirt patched with sweat
drying to salt lines, chilled skin. Faint wood smoke
in the crowded breeze cow bells among the trees
and an iridescent green spider. Seeking in this thronging
vocabulary to think a clear thought about human wrong
which does not disown us. Deceits practised within
necessity. Deceits of the grassy bank. Small
shepherds' huts all over the slopes, secretive hiss
of wind through larches endless forest and mountain
and clouded sky over all, over the oil plants and
railway sidings besides which people survive regimes and
rebellions with luck and custom. Cockchafer climbing
a grass stem, yellow vetch clusters, the earth
written in black ink, hidden under the fuel.

The earth endlessly concealed. Larch top horizons
followed down into the black haze under the mountainside
or the caterpillar's back: the great void of images,
the thought pit, fires glowing in it. Down there
we inhabit this darkness and harvest this blue wheat.
The limestone subsoil that smelts up saxifrage and self-heal.

Valea Rece 2003

for Ivor Gurney

Forgive those warriors brought up in council sheds
and college churchyards who grab the trophies
and kill the loser. Be the proud loser, walk
under the night arches towards a dawn thought,
that these warriors must be forgiven, and respected.

Respect is not enough, they demand allegiance—
"Music is forbidden. It is sinful" and the night walker
digs his grave in the Flemish plain as a slight
blue and peach line opens on the hill edge,
digs into that distance, and hears the dawn birds crackling.
Somebody passed this way 1923 smoking a Players
through the great green of meadows begging for peace
and got home at dawn to a fire in a small room
and a musical praxis that solves nothing outside
of its own moment, for which to live.

And on the other side of the continent the Universal Champions
the thick-set warriors men and women freeze the limbs,
close the shops, blast the currency, and screaming for right
destroy the little we have to be glad of. Screaming for love.
I don't remember ever wanting the world to change.
Walking in grey mornings to the school
and hot afternoons to the bread shop
I learned what had to be learned, bought what I was sent to buy
with what was to spare while the warriors hacked the language.
I heard their thumps and clangs across the town late at night
as I lay in bed, forgave them, and went to sleep.
Common as bread the song of all.

Valea Rece 2003

Szászcsávás: The Older Stratum

Needing new shoes and remembering everything.
The voice shaking but true, treading across the pain.

I'm going to where no one knows me. The strangers,
and the sky with its stars. Don't weep, little mother,
I'll buy you a red scarf with polka-dots.

At night there is nothing, silence of the earth,
impenetrable darkness of the eye, that cannot see
a human face turned up to it or tell the difference
between a turnip and the head of a child with nothing.

I have nothing, I earn nothing, but I have a good time.
I remember only one thing: an oak root under my foot.

And when they arrived, in the early morning,
the star was hidden. The beautiful shining star.

You should see this place in the spring.

Csávás 2003

Long since the stars sank making love possible.
So get on with it, engage the universe, get
out there and walk it in rain and pain in
the grasslands' brilliant costumes the dark lights
gripped in the day's cracks, making love possible.

If love is possible. Heroes crack open the mountains
claiming the time in which we are cancelled. We need
a made thing that stands against this, a gate through
the hissing grass, the great belts of light on the uplands
building hope on thrush heads and their long tunes.

And the stars caught in clefts of rock
white apartment blocks on the far hillside,
you out there, taking the weight, treading the pain,
pushing the air through your teeth to sing love
is indestructible, shield your eyes.

Ceuas de Cîmpie 2003

Pyrenean

The little valley in the foothills
tall birches and twisting stream
snowy crests beyond in sunlight
a marten runs across the road
first thin cherry blossom in the fields
a bell-tower at the crest of each village.

Later sitting on the station platform very cold
suffering pain from an oesophagal hernia
surveying the council houses beyond the track
so like home.

Cathar country, how people survive
or don't and leave a trace in the mind
that survives through centuries, a trace
of defiance, that the world is open, a blue book
wrapped in wool, clutched to the chest
over high and snowy passes.

Four Transylvanian Songs[1]

If you don't work
you won't hear the cuckoo

Or the water
or the wind whistling.

Do the work, saw the log, write the truth
and the cuckoo will sing in the tree

Respect and love the old people
in a world sense

All the work is good
that has good result

Sitting touching the cradle
in the winter.

★ ★ ★ ★

My eyes laugh in your eyes.
My centre hurts for you.

I'm angry with your eyes
looking into mine.

I'm even angrier with your centre
teaching me love.

Whichever way the wind blows
it gets me.

★ ★ ★ ★

My rose, think well of the beginning and the end,
with whom you will cover the world before your eyes.
For it is not borrowed bread which can be given back,
neither is it unearned money which can be spent,
nor is it a hot pillow which you can turn over.
You have found your life's partner, rose,
winter blossom, fallen bud.

    * * * *

    (Dawn song)
I ask unspeaking earth,
silent totality, for help,
to mend the heart
badly broken

And hurting. It is not the heart
but we say heart to describe the hurt.
The earth banging on my coffin lid
will silence all that.

And I'll be a star in the sky
shining faintly at the edge of the sky over the forest
and around midnight I'll poke around the houses
to see what my loves are up to.

    * * * *

[1] Extremely faithful versions in spirit, of anonymous lyrics taken from various CD booklets.

Transylvanian Songs
after Johannes Bobrowski[1]

Father, the great raptor
flies into my chest and makes
his heraldry there.

Grandfather, the dogs bark
Great grandfather, the mud of the road.

The fool, the tourist, runs down the village street
for his camera, disturbing the horses.
The widows sit like crows on the benches.

Their gaze passes through me, fool,
into the distance, to the edge of the forest,
where the orphan bird sits. There the song
makes sense: *at the end of the road*
you will shake hands with the thrush
and the Collectives Officer and the man
from Boston with the GM seeds
all lusting for the black earth.

We walk in rings under the moon. The great
raptor signs our names in the sleep of trees.
Grandfather, across the pastures the river
pours through the stilled mill wheels.
Great grandfather, darkness fills the ground.

---

[1] "Lettische Lieder" in *Sarmatische Zeit* (1961), *Werke*, I, 1987, p.57. Translated as "Latvian Songs", by Ruth and Matthew Mead, *Shadow Lands* (1984). The italicised sentence is quoted from a professional funeral lament from Oltenia, Romania (not in Transylvania) and is part of a prescribed after-life journey.

The Children of Maramureş

A wooden bowl full of blue and red berries,
fresh from the bushes beside the roads, washed of petrol stains.
Take it: love with reason, their eyes say,
therefore hope, without reserve.
Take the gift, accept the reason, lever our hearts over the barricade
with an explanation.

The children stare wide eyed at the strangers
and smile for ever. The day
moulded out of light, the mutual seed,
springs open in time it costs nothing but persistence.
A linking gesture across the border holds the ring dance open to
 the hearth,
where the old ones sit.

Wisps of blue smoke rise from the houses
into the distance. The true moment moves among us,
everyone's work as it works everyone's
fault as it fails, held in the song's return, a hope
balanced on a point of flesh against fate's gerrymandering,
everyone's wish in your tear ever shining

And stabled there. Politicians and clouds
brush the fine heads of the children turned upwards;
a laugh, short and light, rolls down the land,
a reasoned hope in which they turn in the dance, hand on sleeve:
Welcome welcome, bird in the bush, fish in the flood,
futureless presence ringing the earth.

www.ingramcontent.com/pod-product-compliance
Lightning Source LLC
Chambersburg PA
CBHW022008160426
43197CB00007B/328